$36,000 a Year

in Your Own

Home Merchandising Business

$36,000 a Year

in Your Own

Home Merchandising Business

Barry Z. Masser

PARKER PUBLISHING COMPANY, INC.

West Nyack, NY

© 1978 *by*

Parker Publishing Company, Inc.
West Nyack, N.Y.

Library of Congress Cataloging in Publication Data

Masser, Barry Z
  $36,000 a year in your own home merchandising
business.

  Includes index.
  1. Small business--Handbooks, manuals, etc.
2. Self-employed--Handbooks, manuals, etc.
3. Mail order business--Handbooks, manuals, etc.
I. Title.
HF5356.M35   658.8'72   78-4176
ISBN 0-13-918987-4

Printed in the United States of America

HOW THIS BOOK CAN PUT $3,000 IN YOUR POCKET *IN THE NEXT 30 DAYS!*

Does that sound like too much money too quickly? Less than one year ago, Lynn J. thought it was, too. Then she began to market plants that grow wild in her yard — plants she had always considered a nuisance! Now she makes $3,000 a month on them ($36,000 a year), and *more!* This book tells how she does it . . . and how *you* can do it.

This book gives you dozens of breathtaking case histories like that. Before you know it, you'll no longer have any question about your ability to make $3,000 a month. In fact, before you even reach the last chapter, you'll *already* be making yourself over $100 *a day!*

Home merchandising is that kind of dynamite field. And it's incredibly easy to start up with a tiny investment (as you'll find out in the first pages).

$100 a day . . . $3,000 a month . . . $36,000 a year: No matter how you say it, it's the *least* you should expect during your first year in a home business of your own. It's an average taken from a random survey of men and women from all walks of life who are currently engaged in this field as beginners, *without* the benefit of special training, prior experience, or background.

Okay, now that you have an idea about the kind of money you can expect to make in home merchandising, perhaps you wonder about your personal ability to really make it happen. Let's take a look at what it requires:

Can you select novelties and gifts that other people will notice and buy? Yes! You demonstrate a little of that talent every time you enter a store and choose an item. And to help you build that dormant talent of yours, this book provides the secrets and shortcuts used by today's most eminent purchasing professionals. Nancy A., for instance, tells you the details of how she *guarantees* sound buying decisions virtually every time she makes selections!

Can you really become an ingenious merchandiser in just a few days? Yes! Simply follow the same steps developed by America's richest power merchandisers over the past century. When you use these tactics, you'll be playing in the same league as the retailing giants. You'll be a master at creating loss leaders, step-ups, displays that draw huge dollar volume and profits, and many other tricks of the trade. David C., for example, explains how the giving of free gifts has brought him a fortune.

Through numerous experiences of other people, you'll get to know the inner workings of Mail Order (a fabulous $60 billion yearly industry that you can enter *today*!); Direct Sales (responsible for making hundreds of millionaires, and wide open to *you*); Party Plan (one of the world's fastest growing and most profitable businesses, and a sure winner if you like people), and Mobile Showroom merchandising (a sensational new way for you to take your enterprise to where the customers are).

You'll find that one thing you definitely *don't* need for fast success in direct-to-consumer merchandising is sales skill. I repeat: You do *not* need to be a persuasive, fast-talker! You'll read about average people who are now well on their way to personal wealth, and most of them *never sold anything before in their lives!* Modern merchandising techniques all but *eliminate* the need to sell.

So if you are now working as an employee to make someone else rich, or if you are unemployed or under-employed, this book definitely holds the answers that can shift the flow of wealth to *you*. And these answers will bring you earnings of $36,000 a year more easily than you ever imagined possible!

Barry Z. Masser

TABLE OF CONTENTS

*Direct-to-Consumer Marketing: A Fortune Builder Since the
Early 1800's . Today, You Can Operate Any of Four Proven,
Fail-Safe Types of Businesses with Ease . The Cash Profits
Start Flowing Fast and Heavy within Only Days. How George
P. and Family Got a New Camper and Swimming Pool in Six
Amazing Months . Any Mature Adult Can Do It Instantly .
Success Must Come if These Methods Are Followed to the
Letter . You need No Formal Education, No Training, No
Special Skills . All You Must Supply Is a Willingness to Work
Hard in the First Stages . Control Your Income . . . Make as
Much as You Want to Make . You Can Begin a New Life of
Abundance, Freedom and Respect . . . Regardless of Your
Present Situation . How Frank R. Went from Laborer to
Successful Business Operator in 30 Days . How to Use This
Information to Make All Your Dreams of Success a Reality*

4 How Party Plan Merchandising Can Rocket Your Income Practically Overnight . 59

How Jim and Laura J. Kicked Off Their Own Party Plan Business . No Matter Who You Are, the Door to Success is Open . The Anatomy of a Thriving Party Plan Operation . Here's How Easy It is to Get Started in This Extraordinary Business . Your Cash and Supply Requirements . What Sells Fastest at the Biggest Profits . How to Extend Initial Invitations . Room Arrangement Tips That Multiply Sales . How to Dramatize Products for Maximum Sales Punch . Ten Simple Steps for Fabulously Successful Party Sales . How "Game Playing" Magically Creates a Buying Atmosphere . After the First Party, You Simply Sit Back and Rake-In the Cash Profits . Hostess Incentives . . . The Smart Way to Accelerate Your Success . Ten Hours Per Week Yields $18,500 Yearly Income for Mildred A. . The Advantages of Pre-Packing Product Assortments for Your Sub-Distributors . Establishing an Image for Your Rapidly Growing New Business . Doing Big Business with Organizations and Clubs . Arlene P. Tells About a Gigantic Cash Offer for Her New Party Plan Business

5 How Direct Sales Can Bring You the Same Riches It Brought to America's Retailing Giants . 81

One of the Oldest Fortune-Making Businesses in This Country . How Simple It Is to Get Started in a Big, Big Way . A Frank Look at Start-Up Costs . Ken F. Was Floored When His $200 Investment Zoomed to $6,200 in Just Four Months . Getting the Most Out of Your Marketing Area . The Law of Averages Assures Financial Success in the Giant Direct Sales Field . Eight Steps to a Foolproof Presentation . No "Selling" Necessary! Low-Pressure Can Get Consistently Big Dollar Volume and Profits . What to Say and How to Say It for Dramatic Results . How Jim S., Started in Business in the Morning and Counted His First Impressive Profits That Same Afternoon . How to Quickly Blanket Your Community with

1

$36,000 A YEAR IS EASIER THAN YOU EVER DREAMED POSSIBLE

DIRECT-TO-CONSUMER MARKETING:
A FORTUNE BUILDER SINCE THE EARLY 1800's

If you have seen vintage Hollywood westerns on the late show, you're undoubtedly familiar with the rickety peddler's wagons that pushed westward as part of the expanding frontier over a century ago. Aboard these special wagons were the material necessities of life normally unavailable on the plains . . . and a sprinkling of luxury items out of reach to all but the most affluent early Americans.

In the more than one hundred fifty years following that era of merchant and wagon, two distinct and powerful industries evolved: One is the retail store and its suppliers; the other is the direct-to-consumer merchandiser.

This book brings you the big money methods that have been refined by some of the most successful direct merchandisers in America through the decades. While you are engrossed in these fascinating strategies, don't lose sight of this important point: YOUR POTENTIAL FOR WEALTH IS EVERY BIT AS GOOD *TODAY* AS IT WAS FOR THE PIONEERS IN THE GOOD OLD DAYS!

TODAY, YOU CAN OPERATE ANY OF FOUR PROVEN, FAIL-SAFE TYPES OF BUSINESSES WITH EASE

In this day and age, the basic procedure of giving customers a choice of merchandise in the comfort of their own homes remains essentially unchanged from the way it was done in past generations. But there are *more ways* goods can be offered. Let's look at the ways, and at the differences between them:

The Party Plan Method consists of inviting people to a home sales party. Merchandise is displayed on a table, and the operator describes each item for the benefit of the guests present. Such home showings are marked by informality; they are usually as much social events as sales parties. This merchandising method is one of the fastest growing industries in America.

The Direct Sales Method is simply the process of presenting a product line to buyers by bringing items directly to their door. The long success of this merchandising strategy demonstrates beyond any doubt that many, many customers *prefer* to make purchases this way. And experienced direct sales operators know that a certain number of visits to consumers will always result in a given number of sales. This merchandising method can *always* be counted on to produce a steady, far above average income.

The Mobile Showroom Sales Method utilizies a van, truck or automobile trunk to carry products to consumers, usually gathered in large numbers. The operator of a mobile showroom has far greater range than most other direct marketers, and can seek out business on a moment's notice.

The Mail Order Method is the best way to present products to the largest number of consumers in the shortest possible time. It is the most talked about merchandising method, and one of the most exciting. It has the potential for literally overnight wealth . . . *if* the operator follows proven rules—and avoids common pitfalls.

Countless fortunes have been, and are being made today in each of these direct merchandising fields. To say the methods for success have been proven would be understatement. They are virtually *fail-safe*. And they are *easy* when you follow the same well-documented steps used by the best merchandisers.

THE CASH PROFITS START FLOWING FAST AND HEAVY WITHIN ONLY DAYS

Almost any new business can be expected to lose money during the first year or so of operation. Direct-to-consumer marketing is vastly different; *The cash profits generally begin to flow during your very first day of activity!* And they don't stop unless *you* stop.

Why this dramatic difference between direct marketing and most ordinary businesses? Because you go to the customer. There is *no* need to spend huge advertising dollars and hopefully wait for response. There is *no* necessity for you to fret about rain or cold keeping buyers away. There is *no* need for consumers to find you; *you* find them!

The income you make is your choice and your choice alone. A fact that will be repeated several times in this book is that for every ten potential customers, anywhere from one to four of them will make a cash purchase at any given time, wherever they happen to be. These percentages are constant. It is this phenomenon that has made direct merchandising the gigantic industry it is today.

If you're having an off day, perhaps you'll get only one order from every ten people you see. *But the next day could yield five, six, or seven for every ten.* Whatever you desire to put into this business is what you'll get in return, without exception.

If you start your business on the first of the month, you can have $200, $500, $1000, or more, by the tenth. The people in your neighborhood and in your city are buying every day of the week. The moment you decide to get a big share of that spending, it's yours for the asking!

HOW GEORGE P. AND FAMILY GOT A NEW CAMPER AND SWIMMING POOL IN SIX AMAZING MONTHS

We spoke in the back yard of George's suburban home. The youngsters floated on rafts in the pool while their mother looked on. The big, new swimming pool was the result of his first six months in business. After only half a year in direct merchandising, he was able to pay cash for the pool and a new camper, two expensive luxuries they had been dreaming about for the past eight years or more.

George had been working in a store selling power tools over the counter for twelve years. "I made maybe ten percent more every year since I first started in that job. But instead of getting closer to being able to buy the luxuries we've always wanted, I seemed to be getting further away."

One day George sold a customer a power drill. It wasn't busy in the store, so they got to talking. The man explained that he was in business for himself, and had ten people working for him. Some of them gave home sales parties two or three nights a week, and the others went door to door with a line of small decorative items.

"I was all ears, but then he floored me," related George. "He told me he worked an average of two days a week, and only one or two nights. He said he'd probably make over $40,000 by the end of the year . . . all on the work other people were doing for him! I feel that my life started to change right then and there thanks to that customer."

George got enough information about the man's operation to enable him to try it for himself. He had two weeks vacation time coming, and his wife, Cindy, agreed to take part in the new part-time venture.

During the first few days of George's vacation, he and Cindy looked around at wholesalers' showrooms, importers' displays and auctions. They finally decided to take a nice assortment of brass decorative pieces from Thailand that they had seen in an importer's suite. This dealer gave George and Cindy two big cartons full of merchandise *on consignment,* so it wouldn't cost them a cent until they sold it! Then, Cindy set up a party at their house. She invited friends, neighbors and relatives . . . around twenty-five people altogether. On the evening of the showing, they set up a simple but striking display with the brassware, made coffee, and sat on the edges of their seats waiting for the results.

In less than four hours, they had *netted* $292. To convince themselves it wasn't a fluke, they scheduled another party with a different crowd for the following Thursday evening (many of the guests who attended the first showing brought others for the second one). They did $316 at the follow-up showing! George and Cindy continued in business on a spare time basis for the next three months, and things kept getting better and better. George finally gave notice at work, and the business *really* got going after that.

That was six months ago. Now they have the pool, the camper, and more money that they've ever had before. George had to hire a bookkeeper, and she estimates they will make at least $36,000 this year.

ANY MATURE ADULT CAN DO IT INSTANTLY

George P. and his wife did not accomplish any kind of magic. In fact, they are still astounded at how simple the climb to prosperity has been. George secretly admits to occasional guilt feelings about having so much leisure time at home with his family!

The real ingredient in this story of new-found wealth is this: George P., an average person in every respect, finally realized that working for somebody else would result only in the increased prosperity of that person, his employer. Seeing this, he became receptive to ideas that would allow him to work for his own benefit. When the right idea came along, he grabbed it.

This man, and the countless other women and men who have started successful businesses of their own, invariably seem to follow a similar pattern; they one day decide to devote all of their strength and energy to an enterprise of their own . . . and they simply *do* it!

In almost every instance, these people who reach the top income levels can look back and say that *the challenge was more fun than they've ever had before, and that it was far easier than they had ever expected it would be!*

SUCCESS *MUST* COME IF THESE METHODS ARE FOLLOWED TO THE LETTER

If you consider going into a business that is unusually complex, or one that demands special background, the possibility of encountering difficulty increases. In support of this are studies showing that poor management is the reason for most business failures; the owners get in over their heads and flounder.

If you take a look around you and do some investigating, you'll see that *most* enterprises *are* complex. A small hot dog stand can produce a fortune for its owner, but he or she must be something of a master at preparing food, and should certainly be expert in knowing where to obtain ingredients, how much to order on any given day, how to care for perishables, and so forth.

And there are an infinite number of variables in operating a typical business; the ethnic composition of the neighborhood, the part of the country where the firm will function, the climate, are all elements to consider.

But direct-to-consumer marketing is virtually the same anywhere in America. Furthermore, it is totally uncomplicated. And the best thing about it is that *the rules for successful operation do not vary.* As mentioned earlier, the guidelines have been used in practically the same form for over a century!

Therefore, if you are a mature adult . . . and you are willing to focus your concentration on an enterprise of your own . . . and you are determined to follow the *proven* procedures set forth in this book, there is nothing to stop you from attaining your fondest dreams of wealth.

There are times when the temptation to introduce tactics of your own is overwhelming. Nearly every business owner understands that phenomenon, and must resist the impulse. The ones who succeed in staying with the *known* methods are the big winners.

A football team that finds itself in a dismal slump will immediately return to practicing the *fundamentals* of blocking and tackling. They might later realize that the losing streak was due to small *extra* wrinkles that various players had gradually added to their basic moves; a guard may have been taking an unnecessary half-step, thus letting the opposing defense through the line.

This book does *not* contain vague generalities or nebulous theories about how to run a business. It gives you step-by-step methods that get the job done in no uncertain terms. It actually suggests words you may use that have been used successfully by others in the past. It is absolutely specific about how to make your direct-to-consumer marketing enterprise work, and work *fast*.

By religiously following these methods, you are giving yourself every conceivable head start toward a thriving firm of your own.

YOU NEED NO FORMAL EDUCATION, NO TRAINING, NO SPECIAL SKILLS

$36,000 a year can be as easy for you as reading these pages, then applying the recommended steps. If you're looking for involved formulas that get into high finance, you won't find them here.

So the extent of your formal education doesn't matter in the least. Of course, you should be able to figure simple percentages (helpful when calculating profit margins when you price merchandise). And it can be beneficial to have the ability to write short letters (sometimes useful in finding product sources), but knowledge of academic subjects is simply not needed.

If you have shied away from entering your own business because you lack a college degree, or even a high school diploma, you're on the right track in this field.

Heaven only knows how many good people have hesitated entering marketing fields because they felt it required specialized training. There is little doubt that practice will make you more and more proficient, but you'll get every bit of knowledge you need to begin in this book. You *won't* need courses, seminars, or supervision to reach big earnings.

"Inborn skills" have also been vastly overrated; while it may be true that certain individuals seem to have natural talent for whatever fields they pursue, these fortunate people are few and far between. A more typical situation is one where the person must develop skills in the process of functioning in a certain roll. It takes time for most of us.

Many people have, at one time or another, been intimidated by exceptionally brilliant personalities. The magnetism seems to surround them, and they appear to make things happen in their favor almost at will. That brand of charisma isn't necessary for prosperity in direct marketing. On the contrary, today's consumer appreciates a brief, straightforward approach.

Be *you*. Take the tools nature gave you, and utilize them to the maximum advantage. Don't spend a moment of anxiety about your education, training, or skills, or the lack of them.

ALL YOU MUST SUPPLY IS A WILLINGNESS TO WORK HARD IN THE FIRST STAGES

You must "fill the pipeline" as rapidly as you can after launching your new business. Visualize a big, empty pipe, open at both ends. Before anything of substance can come out of one end, it must be filled to capacity from the other.

In your particular case, the things you fill your pipe with will be contacts with prospective customers, interviews with possible suppliers, and so on. Although you will begin to make cash profits immediately, the big results won't come until the pipeline is jam-packed. Then, every bit of input you provide will quickly lead to something good happening.

This can be accomplished in as little as two weeks. It can take as long as a few months. Therefore, the more work you do during the starting phase of your enterprise, the faster it will reach financial maturity.

Even incredibly fast racing cars require a push to get rolling. You must do that much for your own prosperity.

CONTROL YOUR INCOME . . . MAKE AS MUCH AS YOU WANT TO MAKE

One of the delights of owning your own home merchandising business is being able to make exactly as much as you need or want. Your personal commitment to work can be as great or small as you desire. Again, no boss tells you when or how hard to work.

Any individual who has other responsibilities in life can appreciate this feature, and we all have other obligations to some extent:

Teachers can make *far* more money during the few months of summer vacation than their entire yearly teaching salary would represent. A homemaker busy with raising small children and the numerous other chores required to keep a family going can operate a business two hours a day and easily equal her husband's income. Retired people can work when they feel like it and make enough money to pay for all the things they want.

Part-time and full-time home merchandisers can select income levels that may have seemed unrealistic in the past, and *make* it! If you've been working as a clerk for $8,500 a year, and you suddenly see that a $36,000 annual income is a snap, you might have to pinch yourself a few times before believing it. You have probably been programmed to think of $10,000 or $12,000 a year as your ultimate earning potential. Nonsense!

Now that the tools for prosperity are in your hands, you must get accustomed to thinking of yourself as a big-league money earner. Why *shouldn't* you own the biggest house on the block? Why *not* drive the car of your choice? *What's* so farfetched about a European vacation for you every year? The people who are able to do those things are no better than you are; they have merely followed success steps to the top just as you will do right now!

So pick an income, and *make* it. The title of this book suggests $36,000 because it's realistic, yet begins to approach the "privileged" status. It's an income that you can make by following the steps in this book, and it brings you to the very threshold of wealth.

YOU CAN BEGIN A NEW LIFE OF ABUNDANCE, FREEDOM AND RESPECT . . .
REGARDLESS OF YOUR PRESENT SITUATION

It seems that adversity quite often spawns great accomplishment. When the strength of the human spirit overcomes the severe trials of life, it frequently rises to greater heights than it ever has before. Thus, reverses tend to make people stronger.

No matter what kind of experiences you've had in the past, you are standing now at the beginning of an entirely new life. It's as if the slate has been wiped clean.

If you are down to your last few dollars, the merchandising programs described in this book will show you how to turn that little bit of money into a substantial amount; after a short while, money will never be a problem to you again. On the other hand, if you have had a history of winning, your victories in the past will pale in comparison to the ones that lie ahead.

For most working Americans, a career of holding various jobs has resulted in a disappointing salary. True, this salary paid the rent, bought groceries, and may even have purchased a few luxuries now and then. But when all is said and done, there is little to show for those years of loyalty and dedication. This is depressing. It can give even a strong person feelings that to keep trying is futile. Nothing could be further from the truth.

This story shows how a man rose above the bitterness of wrenching defeat to get everything he ever wanted in life through his own merchandising business.

HOW FRANK R. WENT FROM LABORER
TO SUCCESSFUL BUSINESS OPERATOR IN 30 DAYS

Immediately after graduating from high school, Frank R. became an apprentice for a construction company. It seemed to be everything he wanted: The promise of advancement and eventually a supervisory position; good money once he was finished with training; and work outdoors which was important to him.

He proved to be a capable worker, and he advanced as he expected he would. Frank quickly became a journeyman. He married, and purchased a home soon after.

Although there were minor irritations associated with his trade, such as weather interruptions, occasional strikes and periods of reduced building activity, Frank R. was more than satisfied.

During the beginning of his twentieth year of service, a crisis arose that changed Frank's life. One morning his alarm rang at 5:30 a.m., as it had every morning for years, but he could not reach the clock to turn it off. A searing pain traveled down his back to his right foot in jolting waves. With his wife gently helping, Frank managed to maneuver into a sitting position at the edge of the bed. Several minutes later, as he spoke to the doctor over the phone, he realized that his career in construction had come to an abrupt end.

Examination confirmed damage to a spinal disc. What had been an annoying ache the day before, after lifting a steel structural part, had developed into a disabling condition. Within a week, the pain had subsided to a tolerable level, and Frank had to face the immediate necessity of finding a way to produce income.

While there would be certain payment benefits coming to him that would prevent complete financial disaster, these benefits would in no way compensate for the shocking loss of his career, or maintain the lifestyle he and his family had come to enjoy.

Frank investigated scores of small businesses. He found them to be priced far beyond his financial capability and felt he simply did not possess the skills needed to operate them. He also looked at a number of business opportunity propositions that were, for one reason or another, unsatisfactory.

Depression began to set in, and Frank felt he was in a headlong plunge from which there was no escape. He had never sold anything in his life. He knew nothing else except his original trade. Just at the point where he was on the edge of total despair, an idea came to him. He describes the events that occurred during that crucial time of adjustment:

"I remembered a little truck that would sometimes stop at one of our construction sites. This man had the back loaded with merchandise. He carried novelties, gifts, toys, jewelry, sunglasses, everything you could think of. The fellows working on the site would walk over and buy stuff. They always needed combs and toiletries. And they bought things for their wives and kids, too. I know I saw lots of money change hands every time he came around.

"I *owned* a truck like that one! What would stop me from finding items like those and doing the same thing? All I'd have to do is rig up racks and shelves in the truck, get whatever business license I'd need, and I would be in business for myself!"

It was actually almost as simple as the former construction worker made it sound. Before thirty days had gone by, he and his mobile showroom were busily making the rounds in the city, finding every location where people congregated. Getting merchandise at the right price was easy, and so was displaying it in the truck. He didn't have to sell . . . the items sold themselves.

Success came to Frank fast. He has never felt better, and he never dreamed he would make as much money as he does now.

"The truck brings me net profits of *at least* $390 a week. When I feel like putting in full days, I can make as much as $500. But I'm planning to open a retail showroom that my wife will run. That should put us way over $40,000 a year. I want to personally stay with the truck because I still love to be outside."

HOW TO USE THIS INFORMATION
TO MAKE ALL YOUR DREAMS OF SUCCESS A REALITY

If it isn't clear to you to by now that a fortune is at your fingertips, it never will be. Frank R. had every possible strike against him: a minimum education, no special knowledge of merchandising, and no job experience outside of construction. But he turned his sole asset, a truck, into a new life of affluence and independence.

Now we're going to proceed with showing you precisely *how* fortunes are made and how you can make yours.

You'll discover ways to raise working capital in a matter of hours. If you don't have, at this moment, enough money to pay the rent next month, by the time it's due you'll have that much and considerably more.

You'll find out how to use the skills of other people to gain wealth the same way the richest business operators have done. Using people-power to your personal advantage is the *only* way you can reach the kind of success this book is about.

Then, you'll find step-by-step procedures on expertly operating four powerful direct merchandising businesses. These are the strategies developed by foremost specialists in the field . . . strategies tested and proven over more than a century.

2

THE INVESTMENT IS TINY, AND IT'S AT YOUR FINGERTIPS THIS VERY MOMENT

HOW TO SOLVE YOUR STARTING CASH REQUIREMENT PROBLEM IN A MATTER OF HOURS

Using the amazing cash raising methods described in this chapter, money can *never* be a reason why any reasonably ambitious adult cannot start a direct marketing business.

First of all, your starting capital can be as modest as $200, and possibly less. Secondly, that initial amount grows before your very eyes; within a matter of days, many operators look back and wonder why they were ever concerned about money in the first place! The huge profits that are typical in this industry put financial anxiety far behind you.

31

But we're not talking about days, we're talking about *hours*. You can have more than enough hard cash in your hand to make a strong start in business in mere hours from the moment you decide to begin. You don't need bank connections, rich friends and relatives, or sources of any other kind. You do it *strictly on your own*, independent of anything or anyone. In this way, your ultimate success does *not* depend on somebody else's willingness or ability to help you. And the gains you make belong to you and you alone.

The essence of these money generating methods is the art of quickly converting possessions you probably considered worthless, into substantial cash. It works more effectively than you probably have ever imagined.

THE FABULOUS WORLD OF FLEA MARKETS AND GARAGE SALES

Every weekend in thousands of communities all over America, countless flea markets and garage sales are held at which millions of dollars change hands.

For some people, these are perfect outlets for realizing maximum profits from unwanted personal goods that collect in their homes over a period of years. For others, such events become a regular routine and an important source of income. For you, they can represent an ideal means to finance your new home merchandising business.

The underlying reason for the phenomenal success of flea markets and garage sales is this: Items that are no longer wanted by people and are thus next to worthless in their eyes are sought by others who are *eager* to pay top dollar for the castoffs. Here are just a few examples of items that traditionally sell quickly:

1. *Nostalgia articles* attract scores of avid buyers; anything you own that looks like it came from a past generation will sell for high prices.
2. *Clothing* in good condition that no longer fits family members is very much in demand.
3. *Household and automobile tools* are always sought by shoppers.
4. *Furniture,* even if broken, goes fast at sales.

5. *Used toys* always command tremendous attention.
6. *Second hand sports equipment* is usually popular.
7. *Electronics items* like radios, TV sets, and tape recorders are generally grabbed by bargain hunters.

The compulsion to find interesting and sometimes valuable articles like the ones listed above draws throngs of shoppers to private homes, drive-in theaters, unoccupied sports stadiums, abandoned supermarkets, and any other facility large enough to house hundreds of temporary display booths.

The market is so vast, and its appetite so varied, that anything from a broken armchair to a pound of cashew nuts will sell and sell fast. The most outlandish merchandise finds buyers aplenty at flea markets and garage sales.

Rental of a display space for one day at a flea market runs in the area of six dollars. The process is as simple as loading your car, and a trailer if necessary, with all the items you have accumulated over the years. You then drive to the market location early in the morning, and attractively display everything you want to sell on folding tables. A garage sale is held in front of your residence (not necessarily in your garage). Handmade signs can be posted around your neighborhood publicizing the event.

HOW MUCH YOU CAN MAKE
IN JUST A FEW SPARE WEEKEND HOURS

Let's take a close look at the results Mary C. and her husband, Paul got during a single weekend. The figures are *typical* of what hundreds of people do every weekend all over the country.

Mary and Paul planned a garage sale for a Saturday, reasoning that passing cars and pedestrians on their way to a nearby shopping center would be attracted to their front yard display of used items. They had the items arranged on tables by 8:00 a.m. At 7:30 p.m. that same evening, the final sales results were these:

2 table lamps .... $ 8.50
Clock radio 7.00
Old manual typewriter 6.50
Upholstered chair 8.00
Sofa 35.00

Various clothing items	18.00
Assorted hand tools	14.70
Two-slice toaster	5.00
Child's portable stroller	5.00
2 automobile tires	9.00
3 framed prints	6.90
Manual lawn mower	6.00
Large mirror	10.00
Office desk	20.00
Desk chair	7.00
4 leather purses	10.50
27 books	15.20
Three-speed boy's bike	12.00
2 porcelain statuettes	5.65
Set of loudspeakers	6.95
Small chest-type freezer (not operating)	21.00
Chest of drawers	20.00
Five-piece card table set	20.00
Camera	15.00
Three-piece set of luggage	9.75
Set of stainless steel flatware	11.00
Portable hair dryer	5.95
40-50 odds and ends	87.80
Total for the Day	**$407.30**

Mary had some concern about rounding up enough merchandise for the flea market they had planned to sell at on the following day, but a concerted search of the house yielded an additional carload of forgotten treasure. Sunday saw them heading toward the market bright and early, the tail-end of their borrowed panel truck jammed to capacity with castoffs of every description.

Eight hours netted Mary and Paul *$294.50 more*! Profits for the two days totalled $701.80 . . . *more* than enough to launch their new direct marketing business.

These people didn't sell a single piece they would miss in the least. Every item was taking up needed space and gathering dust. True, some of it had sentimental value, but not nearly enough to justify keeping—especially in view of the fact that the original $701.80 they collected over that weekend grew to a big $4,877.40 during the next *thirty-six days*—just over *one month* from the day they started their home merchandising activities!

While the results this couple obtained were certainly spectacular enough, they were still rather average in terms of the experiences of hundreds of people every weekend. A case related later in this chapter describes two days of cash raising that can only be termed incredible, though true.

SEARCH YOUR BASEMENT, ATTIC, AND EVERY OTHER NOOK AND CRANNY FOR HIGH-PROFIT CASTOFFS

Any seasoned flea market seller will tell you that one of the secrets of success is to take a long, hard look at your possessions. This should be done without emotion or sentiment. The items you have purchased and received as gifts over the past ten years or more—that you *think* you are hopelessly attached to—must be ruthlessly evaluated as to their continued usefulness to you.

If you're like most people, the things you actually use on a regular basis probably comprise less than ten percent of your total possessions. Everything else, we *hope* to use some day. Or, we feel we may grow to like certain articles despite the fact that we intensely disliked them from the day we first saw them a long time ago. Every item that fails your tough appraisal is a candidate for your flea market or garage sale display.

Every room must be turned upside down, especially those that tend to become storage areas. For example, an infrequently used utility room might have shelves loaded with old boxes containing heaven knows what. The dark corners of closets invariably hold forgotten surprises that you may recall abhoring, but that would delight some shopper. It bears repeating that just because *your* heart doesn't beat faster when you gaze upon some bizarre old gift doesn't mean someone else's won't.

DISPLAY TRICKS THAT DRAW BIG CROWDS OF SHOPPERS

Here are the words of Scott C., an occasional flea market seller:

"The first time I displayed, I finished the day with only $95 in sales. I wasn't really disappointed, but I knew that other people were doing much better, and I wanted to know the reasons why.

"After I did some snooping around on the following Sunday, certain things became clear to me; I found out that you just can't dump items haphazardly on a table, sit down, and expect fantastic sales. The people who did the biggest business were the ones who had interesting displays, action and color.

"I went all out the following week. Pennants, balloons, banners, and signs went up all over my area. I even used a gaudy print fabric to cover my display table. The difference was amazing! I took in over $200 that day, and it's been getting better ever since."

Scott C. discovered some of the basic secrets of good merchandising and display. Regardless of the field in which you choose to operate, effective display is a first essential. The following tactics can be used to dramatic effect at flea markets and in any other type of merchandising you ever do:

1. Use one or more "attention getters." These are items primarily intended to attract attention. The more unusual and remarkable they are, the better. One flea market operator kept a four foot tall replica of a guillotine in front of his display. It wasn't for sale because it was too valuable in drawing curious customers to his space (more about this later).

2. Color should be introduced wherever possible. Don't hesitate to use knockout hues and patterns. Drab displays simply are not appealing.

3. Motion can be extremely helpful. Balloons and small flags that flap and bob in the breeze consistently beckon to passers-by. A battery operated lazy susan loaded with jewelry and other small items rotates invitingly and stops the roving eye of the shopper.

4. Make your display sharp! Clean items to the best of your ability before putting them on display. It stands to reason that shiny articles will appear more valuable than dingy, dusty ones.

The thing is, you must have *flair* to do the maximum amount of business possible. You must be distinctive and different or you get lost in the midst of scores of other displays all around you. By putting just a few moments of thought and preparation into the points described above, you'll be heads above your competition, and you'll reach your financial goal in one, short weekend.

MORE ABOUT ATTRACTING ATTENTION
BY DISPLAYING THE COLORFUL AND UNUSUAL

A restaurant and motel operator located on a desolate stretch of highway running through the desert has a bigger-than-life cement dinosaur standing on the grounds, in clear view of passing motorists. It draws hundreds of tourists weekly, and it has for years.

A fast food restaurant hired a clown for its slow days. The clown, waving people into the restaurant, easily tripled the normal receipts. The owner of an ice cream truck decided to play a simple tune over a loudspeaker as he rolled along his usual route. His business instantly zoomed.

A somethat more subtle variation on attracting attention was the diamond salesman who pulled on an elegant pair of white kid gloves before showing samples of his stones to jewelers. These theatrics rapidly made him the top money-maker in the entire company.

If you plan to use a flea market or garage sale as a method for raising the initial investment for a home merchandising business of your own, do it with a splash!

HOW TO PRICE AND BARGAIN FOR QUICK,
PROFITABLE SALES

People shop at flea markets and garage sales to get bargains. Therefore, your objective is to make them think they're getting just that. The best possible way to create a bargain illusion is to let them successfully argue with you about price.

It's simple enough to accomplish this by giving items away at extremely low prices. But we want to satisfy the customer, and still maintain a decent profit margin. An acceptable profit is 50%, a respectable profit is 100%, and a hefty profit is 150%, or better.

Before you can intelligently establish a pricing policy, you should determine a base cost price for every item you plan to sell. This provides a starting point from which you can build a profit structure. For example, if you paid $10 for a folding chair ten years ago, you might set its cost price at $3.00. (This example is arbitrary. The actual price you set would depend on the item's age, condition, and estimated appeal to the shopper.)

If the chair is in perfect shape, and you feel it represents a good find, mark it up 150%, or $7.50 ($3.00 plus $4.50). If it's fair, mark it up 100%, or $6.00. Try to make *all* of your estimated base costs fair and reasonable. Remember, you have used the items for years, or they have been of absolutely no use to you and are merely taking up needed space.

If, in your judgment, an item is of extraordinary appeal, you can go above 150%. Certain products increase in value over the years, and you should take that into consideration.

Now, since you're willing to operate at a minimum margin of 50%, you have a built-in cushion for bargaining; every article is marked up *at least* 100% over your estimated base cost, and you can drop down to as low as 50% over. Therefore, the $7.50 chair can be sold for $4.50, if necessary. That's a neat profit for you, and a slam-bang buy for the customer, who feels like an expert negotiator.

When items are clearly pre-priced, shoppers are generally far more comfortable. But there is some danger that margins of 150% will frighten them away. So you should make every effort to indicate that the price is subject to reduction. If somebody is admiring the chair, but is obviously hesitating, you can tell them you're willing to part with it for $5.95, or some other lower figure than the tag reads. In many cases, customers who are not shy will *offer* lower prices than your tags show. If such an offer is within your 50% profit guideline, you can accept.

An alternate method to pre-tagging each item is to have a list handy that itemizes each item and its price as you established it. This also gives a degree of comfort to shoppers since they know you're not inventing a price based on their desire to own the article.

"Splitting the difference" works beautifully. If a shopper happens to offer $3.00 for your $7.50 chair, you can quickly reply with a compromise of $5.25, or half the difference between $3.00 and $7.50. Above all, remain flexible. don't refuse reasonable offers. The more cash you earn now, the faster you'll make the *big* money in direct merchandising.

THE INVESTMENT IS TINY, AND IT'S AT YOUR FINGER TIPS   39

RICHARD L. TELLS HOW HE CAPITALIZED HIS
NEW BUSINESS IN TWO AMAZING WEEKENDS

The purpose of this chapter has been to show you how to get your hands on enough money within 48 hours to start your own home merchandising business. For some people, this short-term effort is so stunningly successful, it boggles the mind. Richard L. is such a person.

He planned two consecutive weekends of going to flea markets, mixed in with holding garage sales. He dug up everything he owned that was no longer needed, plus tons of stuff from friends and neighbors. Richard even picked up some saleable items that people in the neighborhood were ready to throw away. His house and garage were bulging.

People came in droves. While Richard was displaying out at the flea market, his wife was selling at home, and received offers for everything in sight; she was collecting money so fast she couldn't even count it properly! By that evening, their pooled income was $2,170!

Richard was in his own business by the third weekend. He had far more money than he needed because his starting investment was only $355. Within the first six months of operation, he had made $17,590. He projects an easy $36,000 yearly income through direct sales and mail order.

And it all started from just two weekends of selling castoffs!

MAKING EVERY DOLLAR OF YOUR NEW CASH RESERVE
PRODUCE UP TO A TWENTY-FOLD PROFIT

So far, we've been dealing in small figures. Using flea markets and garage sales to raise capital simply shows that *anybody*, regardless of his or her present circumstances, can easily finance a lucrative home merchandising business.

Now we'll get into *big* numbers; the kind of money that only certain business owners and top executives make. The key to making an income in that category is for you to first become reasonably proficient in direct merchandising, then to *build an organization that does the work FOR you.*

Anybody can make a living, even an exceptionally good one, operating merchandising programs by himself. But your earnings *multiply* when others are out there selling for your direct benefit. It has the same effect as making every dollar of your initial investment grow ten, fifteen, even twenty times in just a few weeks.

This stupendous growth potential means a $200 start could grow to $4,000 in 30 to 60 days. If you re-invested only $1,000 of that in your business, you could expect it to grow to $20,000 in another 60 days. And with each passing month, your organization becomes larger and stronger. The figures get to be astronomical when you master the art of recruiting people to do the work for you. The following pages show you how to harness that enormous wealth-building power.

3

HOW TO BUILD A MONEY MACHINE THAT PRODUCES GIANT INCOME WHILE YOU RELAX AT HOME

THE SECRET OF THE SUPER RICH: OTHERS MAKE THE MONEY FOR YOU

You can be fairly sure that the day of the self-made individual, wrestling with the world and wringing a fortune out of it with his bare hands, is over. No matter how hard or how intelligently you work, the odds are against your making sizable wealth all by yourself.

A well-established direct marketing enterprise *can* give you phenomenal income when you operate it alone. But to reach truly astonishing wealth—and the kind of personal freedom that permits you to take long vacations, sleep late, and do whatever you please—requires that you make use of people who do the job for you.

The overwhelming majority of men and women who have built financial empires have done it through the efforts of others. The harnessing of human energy is their secret of success. These astute people discovered very early in the game that most of us are perfectly content to make a modest buck in return for an honest day's work. The average worker aspires only to small raises, microscopic bonuses and promotions that merely provide more impressive titles. The wealthy have made it by using these average people.

Therefore, understanding the business of utilizing people for your own purposes is the key to wealth.

But before you can set about the task of employing others to the goal of enriching you, it is vitally important that you have a viable program to give your recruits. The only practical way to attract people to work for you is to provide them a way to make money. While they are making themselves a living, they are making you a fortune.

The programs you will offer your recruits are the merchandising methods described in this book. But before you can expect others to operate them successfully on your behalf, you should spend some time practicing them yourself. As soon as you are comfortable with your own knowledge of their workings, you can begin to build your organization, and thus *your own* financial empire.

BUILD YOUR WEALTH BY DRAWING FROM 30 MILLION OR MORE AMERICAN OPPORTUNITY SEEKERS

One of the most extraordinary facets of American life is the enormous number of people looking for ways to make extra money. This vast segment of our population has made more millionaires than any other identifiable market. If you can reach these opportunity seekers with a money-making plan, you will almost certainly prosper.

The thousands of people living in your community who are searching for extra income are, obviously, the group you must target for in your own quest for wealth. They might be housewives looking for ways to make money in return for a few hours work. Some are retirees anxious to supplement pensions. A portion are known to be full-time employees willing to give their evening hours for side income. Many are people who simply do not qualify for positions in the normal job market, and who would be extremely receptive to an offer of full-time employment you could make them.

Opportunity seekers come in myriad sizes, shapes, colors, and descriptions. They live in every community, rich and poor alike. They may be at any level of intelligence or mental agility. There is no way to make any hard and fast rules about what they say or how they look. The only thing you can be sure of is the fact that they want to find a source of dollars; this one unchanging fact gives you everything you need to find them.

People searching for income angles tend to read certain kinds of newspapers and magazines. They generally respond to a certain type of language and appeal. So we have a situation where their desire to earn extra money makes them highly visible . . . and vulnerable to our offer of chances at wealth.

We will thoroughly discuss a number of highly effective, proven ways to reach these people, thus setting the stage for your own climb to the top.

SUB—DISTRIBUTOR RECRUITMENT TECHNIQUES THAT GET QUICK RESULTS

Your skill at recruiting sub-distributors, then, will play a major role in how fast you prosper. For that reason, you should make every effort to stay with methods that have worked for some of the biggest operators in merchandising.

The recruitment procedure is amazingly simple. It's a three-step method, as follows:

Step one is the placement of a simple, straight-forward classified ad. The purpose of this ad is to *get the response of an individual looking for a way to make money.*

This is so important, it deserves additional description: The ad is placed *only* for the purpose of making an opportunity seeker visible to you. The ad must *not* give details about your offer. The only way you'll successfully build an organization of straight commission sub-distributors is by dealing with the recruits *after* they have demonstrated initial interest by answering your ad.

The ad you should run must impart this basic message:

> WOMEN/MEN—MAKE BIG MONEY
> FROM YOUR HOME. MERCHANDISE
> AND EVERYTHING ELSE YOU NEED IS
> SUPPLIED!
>
> (Your name here . . . phone number here)

The downfall of most unsuccessful recruitment ads is that they give *too much* information. Whatever you do, *resist* the temptation to tell your entire story in an ad that should be used only to get you in contact with prospective sub-distributors.

The strategic placement of your classified ad is most important. It was earlier mentioned that certain types of magazines and newspapers are popular with opportunity seekers. You should use *only* those particular publications. The guidelines for recognizing them are as follows:

1. The BUSINESS OPPORTUNITIES classification in the local newspaper in your city can be effective *if* it normally carries a substantial amount of other classified advertising. The advantage of using a local newspaper is that you will attract people who live in your community—where you want to get established initially—rather than nationally, which can come later. When you are ready for expansion, certain magazines are ideal.

2. Money is generally mentioned in the titles of the magazines we want to use, and the contents deal exclusively with making money. They contain articles about various business opportunities, and thus appeal to the people we are after.

3. These magazines are heavily used by mail order advertisers. There are pages and pages of ads for a wide variety of products and services.

4. In almost every case, the cover of a magazine in this category includes an actual picture of cash as part of the overall design.

5. There are several weekly and bi-weekly tabloid newspapers sold near supermarket checkout stands and in

drugstores. These are also powerful in our market. They carry a large number of mail order ads as the magazines do, and they usually include strong classified sections.

The second step of your recruitment procedure is the handling of the inquiry you will receive from an interested opportunity seeker. This will be a telephone conversation, the person calling you to get more information about your deal. Remember, you should give only enough information over the phone to keep the person's interest at a high level (a suggested procedure for handling prospects is covered later in this chapter).

Step three, the face-to-face interview, is when you tell your complete story. Here again, by using the methods that have proved successful for the biggest merchandisers in the industry, you will get as many sub-distributors as you need. These methods for effective interviews are also examined in detail a little later in this chapter.

OTHER POWERHOUSE METHODS YOU CAN USE THAT ATTRACT TOP, COMMISSIONED SALESPEOPLE

Classified ads are by no means the only way to reach the vast business opportunities market. Here are three other methods that are highly regarded for their effectiveness in attracting ambitious recruits:

1. If you decide to develop a mail order business in conjunction with your other direct marketing programs, or if you create your own product catalog for distribution to consumers, a flyer can be developed that offers your customer an opportunity to become a sub-distributor. This recruitment ad could be inserted in the mailer, the catalog, or both. Such a piece might be as simple as a single sheet printed on one side. Figure 1 shows a possible format.

2. One of the most powerful ways to build an organization is by getting to know your customers and finding out which ones would be likely candidates for sub-distributorships. During the day-to-day operation of your direct marketing activities, certain customers will show extreme interest in your products. You can casually mention to these people the fact that your business is growing rapidly, and you

MAKE SPARE TIME $$$ AT HOME

Dear Customer:

Here's an incredible opportunity for a high-profit merchandise distribution business of your own. You can work when you feel like it...and begin earning big money immediately!

Smith Distributors needs an independent dealer in your area. NO selling is required! You simply use the same money-making methods that have made us one of the fastest-growing businesses in town. You need NO long training period; we'll teach you everything you need to know in a matter of hours!

This once-in-a-lifetime opening is available to mature women and men of all ages. And NO INVESTMENT IS REQUIRED! Smith Distributors supplies everything you need to get started, and it doesn't cost you a penny until your first big orders come in.

CALL TODAY for the exciting details and get started toward prosperity!

Sincerely,

R.J. Smith

R.J. Smith
(000) 000-0000

Figure 1

have need for additional representatives to show products and make extra money. Several of the most successful direct operators use this method exclusively and never fail to add five to ten new sub-distributors to their organizations every month!

3. Many large apartment complexes—and almost every major supermarket—have bulletin boards that carry messages for those interested. A single 3" x 5" card such as shown in Figure 2 tacked to dozens of these boards will get you results.

MAKE BIG MONEY FROM YOUR HOME PART-TIME!

Everything you need is supplied at *no cost*!

Call Mrs. Smith, 000-0000

Figure 2

By using any or all of these proven recruitment methods, you should generate a constant flow of people anxious to make money for themselves . . . and for *you*. The following pages describe highly effective ways to deal with prospective recruits on the phone and during the personal interview that follows.

HOW TO HANDLE PHONE INQUIRIES FROM PROSPECTIVE SUB-DISTRIBUTORS

As stressed earlier, you must avoid giving information to interested people when they call you in response to any of the recruitment ads just described. No matter how anxious they are to get details, this *must wait* until you meet them personally.

When potential recruits call, your end of the conversation must be limited to the following points:

1. Before anything else, get the person's name and telephone number.

2. Introduce yourself and your company name, if appropriate. Then, immediately tell the caller that the opening still exists, and that you recommend an interview at the earliest possible time. This meeting should be ar-

ranged within the following twenty-four hours. This will assure you of speaking to the prospect while his interest is at the highest level.

3. Normally, the phone conversation will end here; immediately after a mutually convenient time has been agreed upon. If, however, the prospect persistently asks questions, make every effort to confine your end of the discussion to the following two areas:

4. There is *no* investment required, and nothing to purchase initially if he or she is lucky enough to be selected.

5. The opportunity *is* spectacular, and the income potential *is* enormous.

6. One effective way to prevent being drawn into a conversation that will reduce your chances of getting an interview is to tell the prospect that your phone is ringing off the hook, and you *must* cut it short and take care of other callers.

7. Tell the person you are looking forward to the interview and hang up.

WHAT TO SAY DURING THE INTERVIEW
TO GET MAXIMUM RECRUITING RESULTS

The interview is where the full impact of your offer should be delivered. Your complete merchandise line should be displayed, plus any catalogs or mailers you have created. The time has come to impress your prospect by using every means at your disposal.

The biggest weapon in your arsenal is *profits;* the only reason your prospect has arrived for the interview is to find out how much money can be made in your enterprise, and how it's done. Therefore, after you have exchanged the usual pleasantries, you should get right down to the business of describing what it's all about.

First, tell your prospect that your are operating a successful direct marketing business, that there is no need to sell, and that you need help keeping up with the demand for your products.

Next, launch directly into a description of the profit potential. The best way to approach this is graphically; you might prepare a simple chart that shows how easy it would be for the representative to earn $2,500 per month and more by working just a few hours each week. The figures you actually show the prospect would depend, of course, on how much spread there is between the sub-distributor's purchase price from you, and the selling price of the item. A sample chart is shown later that can be used as a pattern for one of your own.

Another extremely hard-hitting point you should make is the no-investment feature of your offer, if indeed you decide to use it. This arrangement provides that you supply a basic group of product samples to each new sub-distributor at no charge. The items are *consigned* to the representative, and must either be paid for or returned to you eventually. A consignment agreement like the one shown in Figure 3 must be signed by your new representative.

Date:_____

*(sub-distributor's name)*_____ agrees to return the items listed above to____ *(your name)*____ upon request. It is further agreed that all items not returned will be purchased at the prices indicated above. All products are to be maintained in good condition until returned or purchased.

_____
(sub-distributor's signature)

Figure 3

This agreement should appear just below an inventory list that itemizes each product you consigned to your new representative. It also shows the price you charge for each item.

While it's true such an arrangement will cost you a little extra for samples, it will also serve the purpose of making your offer exceedingly attractive to people with no money to invest. The no-investment feature puts you far ahead of competition in terms of appeal. Your representatives can take orders from their consigned samples and order the sold items from you. Thus, they don't pay anything until *after* orders are received from their customers.

If you don't wish to use the consignment concept, an alternative is to charge new recruits a token amount for a "starter package" that includes items samples, order forms, and so forth.

The actual amount you charge could cover the cost of the samples. Some operators make this nominal amount refundable on the first order obtained by the new sub-distributor.

At this point in the interview, show the prospect your product line. Mention the fact that you'll be busy acquiring fast-selling new items in order to keep the line interesting and competitive. Also assure the person that you'll provide continuing assistance in every way possible to help him prosper as you have.

THE IRRESISTIBLE MONEY-MAKING OPPORTUNITY YOU CAN OFFER

When you show a prospective sub-distributor figures like these, you are presenting a business proposition that is simply too good to miss. This particular chart is for "party plan" operations; it shows a scale of weekly profit results based on the number of showings held. If every showing grossed just $200, and your sub-distributor made 40%, Figure 4 shows how it would look.

Number of parties in one week	1	3	6	10	12
Sub-distributor's weekly profits	$80	$240	$480	$800	$960

Figure 4

This is *not* taking into consideration the money that can be made by the sub-distributor in a few hours of direct sales each week *in addition* to home sales parties . . . not to mention the enormous profits that could result from a simultaneous mail order program!

Your recruit should also understand that many of the profits are *automatic*; mail order brings in cash just by sending out a catalog or flyer. Party plan produces big income merely by coordinating get-togethers where products are displayed. Therefore, *the sub-distributor is prospering through the efforts of others just as you are!*

And the repeat business can be astounding. After several weeks, the orders come in effortlessly. Your sub-distributor would be earning more than ever before, and multiplying *your* profits while you stand back and watch!

HOW TO DIVIDE PROFITS
THE WAY BIG-TIME OPERATORS DO IT

There are several important factors to remember when establishing your profit structure:

1. Sufficient profits for *you* from the efforts of your sub-distributors.
2. The ability of your sub-distributors to make money for themselves.
3. A competitive selling price on your product line.

Here's the anatomy of a suggested profit structure on a $5.00 item:

$ 5.00	Your cost on an item (the price you pay a supplier)
2.00	40% (your profit from a sub-distributor)
7.00	Sub-distributor price (The amount he or she pays you for the item)
11.95	Retail selling price (the amount your sub-distributor gets from the consumer)
4.95	Net profits to your sub-distributor . . . **over 70%**

Thus, you make a hefty 40% on all merchandise you supply to your sub-distributors. They, in turn, can make over 70% on their sales at full retail. But if they want to discount, they can reduce their prices considerably and *still* make 40% without difficulty.

You can increase your percentage and cut the potential profit of your sub-distributor, but any experienced direct marketer will tell you that a strong organization is built faster if your people are making good money.

HOW BETTY R. GOT FIFTEEN AMBITIOUS PEOPLE
TO DO HER SELLING AFTER ONLY TWO WEEKS IN BUSINESS

This young mother soared to financial success so rapidly and unexpectedly, she *still* can't believe it really happened!

It started when Betty R., a homemaker, learned that a local textile wholesaling firm was planning to close-out several hundred small area rugs that were not selling well in department stores. She contacted the company with the intention of purchasing six rugs for her own residence, but ended up buying a gross—with an option on two remaining gross.

The moment she saw the colorful little rugs, Betty was sure they would be popular with women who would use them for accents in various rooms. At the close-out price, she could offer tempting values and still more than double her investment.

She immediately invited her friends and neighbors to see the rugs. Ten people not only made purchases, but they asked Betty if *they* could offer them to people *they* knew! A consignment plan was quickly devised; each woman took twenty rugs to sell. Betty called the wholesaler and exercised her option on the balance of his rug stock.

In the space of two weeks, she still had the original ten women busily selling rugs, plus five others who wouldn't take no for an answer. Betty was making a net profit on each rug of $2.25, and her fifteen sub-distributors had gone through 432 rugs in another week . . . the entire three gross was sold out in three weeks! Her total profit was $972.

Although the close-outs were gone, she was still able to buy a similar rug at favorable prices from the wholesaler. But in addition to rugs, Betty R.'s product line had expanded to gifts of every imaginable kind. In three months her weekly income was up to an average of $480, and growing fast!

Betty had never made a single personal sale outside of those to her original fifteen women. By supplying them with competitively priced, attractive products, she could easily reach an income of well over $35,000 in her first year as a direct marketer. And Betty would never have to do anything else except the thing she loved to do most: buy!

Such is the power of having others do the work.

TRAINING: TWO HOURS PER WEEK
FOR EACH NEW REPRESENTATIVE

There is probably no other business in the world that yields such gigantic profits with such small effort on the part of the owner.

Direct marketing is so utterly simple, it can be done—and done well—by practically anyone. This means that the time demands on you are absolutely minimal. By devoting a mere two hours a week to each new recruit, you can be sure of having excellent representation and optimum sales results.

The points you should cover during this two hours of training are as follows:

1. Review the product line. Be sure your sub-distributor understands all the features of each item, construction highlights, and any other important information.
2. Find out what the sub-distributor has been encountering during visits to consumers. If he or she is running into problems, help find a remedy.
3. Get as much information as you can about what the buying public wants. Your sub-distributors can be valuable sources for this vital data. By keeping your ears open and making your people aware of trends, your line will always be well-received by consumers.
4. Every time you meet with a sub-distributor, arrange to have information that will be beneficial. Much of this can come from your *other* representatives. It can pertain to effective things to say to customers, new ways to show items, and so forth.

While the purpose of these training sessions is to make your sub-distributors as productive as possible, the meetings should be pleasant and as brief as you can make them.

BUILDING A PROFIT MACHINE THAT CAN GROW TO STAGGERING SIZE WHILE YOU STAND BACK AND WATCH

So far, we've discussed a way for you to rapidly build an organization that can bring you wealth in merchandising. It requires that you do the recruiting and training. We will now describe a way for you to create *a profit machine that builds itself* . . . that lets you travel the world, or do anything you please . . . without the need to personally sell anything or recruit anyone!

As soon as you have established a small, dependable organization of sub-distributors, select a few of the very best ones to become district managers. Tell these few people that they are free to recruit as many salespeople of their own as they wish within their defined districts. Explain to them that they will make 20% on the sales produced by their new recruits *in addition* to their usual personal production.

Here again, a chart will dramatize the potential. It can show each district manager recruiting and training ten new people and each new individual grossing $250 per week. The total *extra* income for your district manager is an astounding *$500 a week PLUS the* profits from his regular personal sales! (The extra 20% comes from a restructuring of your profit system; 10% can come from your share, and 10% may comfortably be added to selling prices on merchandise).

Such a system can give you statewide coverage in short months and nationwide sales not long after that. This method, in combination with recruitment advertising in national magazines, can make your business blossom into an industry giant in no time.

Let's look at it in terms of *your* income. If, for example, you have divided your city into districts, and each one has a manager and five salespeople producing $250 per week in sales, Figure 5 shows how much you can make depending on the number of districts you have (remember, you make 40% on managers, 30% on the salespeople under them).

Number of districts	1	3	5	8	12	15
Gross sales in one week	$1,500	$4,500	$7,500	$12,000	$18,000	$22,500
Your personal profits in one week	$ 475	$1,425	$2,375	$ 3,800	$ 5,700	$ 7,125

Figure 5

Therefore, if you had only *three* districts in full swing, your annual income, without leaving your home, would be $74,100! That's why $36,000 a year is *conservative* in this remarkable business!

DYNAMIC EXPANSION IS SIMPLE
AND VIRTUALLY AUTOMATIC

The trigger that ignites expansion is the *management layer:* Salespeople will redouble their efforts if they know there is a possibility of achieving the position of district manager. Those who already are district managers will recruit people as fast as they can realizing that each new sales person will produce more dollar volume that will result in fatter commissions.

The built-in incentives in such a system guarantee you an income that multiplies day after day, month after month, indefinitely. Your ceiling is limited only by the quantity of merchandise you can obtain. Your geographic boundaries are limited only by the distances merchandise can be shipped to new districts you have established.

As long as there are millions upon millions of people searching for money-making opportunities, this business strategy will remain a fast track to riches for virtually any ambitious man or woman willing to commit himself to it. When the immense energy and resources of *people* are harnessed as they are by industry leaders, wealth suddenly comes into easy reach.

HOW PAT S. STARTED A CHAIN REACTION
THAT TOOK HIS BUSINESS NATIONAL IN 30 DAYS

Pat S. was flying to a neighboring city on a merchandise buying trip. He had started his own home merchandising business only one week earlier.

The gentleman in the seat next to him was friendly, and in the course of conversation explained to Pat that he was a salesman of industrial supplies. When Pat described his new business, the salesman, Joe V., insisted they spend more time talking after they arrived at the destination. After landing, they found a booth at the terminal coffee shop and proceeded to plan a national merchandise distribution company!

Joe explained that he knew top salespeople in 25 cities in the southern U.S. These people, he said, simply wanted a reliable product source and the chance to make money for themselves. Several previous affiliations had been unsatisfactory because of skimpy commission setups and uncertainty about item availability. Pat assured his new associate that these areas would not present problems in the future.

The prime condition of an agreement, said Pat, was that Joe be made regional sales director. Joe would then make his acquaintances district managers in key cities. They, in turn, would create sales organizations within these cities and surrounding districts. The deal was concluded.

The following day, Pat ordered products based on his new needs, and had samples drop-shipped to addresses provided by Joe.

During the following weeks, there were dozens of phone calls between cities, and a few areas of confusion. But in four weeks from the date it started in business, this young giant of a firm had produced *$5,292 in personal income* for Pat S. and promised to make him an annual income of at least $75,000 the first year! It covered nearly one third of the country and was growing daily!

HOW TO GUARANTEE FAT CASH RETURNS
FROM EACH SUB-DISTRIBUTOR WITH NO RISK TO YOU

There are two widely accepted methods used in getting your sub-distributors off to good starts. One, the merchandise consignment plan, has been covered. It requires that you supply a basic product selection to each recruit with no initial cost to that person. Although the individual must sign a consignment agreement specifying that the items must be returned to you or purchased, this method still is not free from risk.

The prominent advantage of consigning samples is that your offer becomes extremely attractive; the recruit can begin to make money before paying anything at all to you. The obvious drawback in this plan is that people will vanish with your samples from time to time, and you're stuck with the loss. This shouldn't happen often, but it can occur.

The no-risk method, which is also rather popular, requires payment from your recruit for samples and other materials you supply in the starter package. While the ten, fifteen, or twenty dollars you charge will, indeed, protect you from loss, it might also discourage a certain number of people from becoming sub-distributors. One of the ways around this is to agree to fully refund the initial charge when the sub-distributor submits his first order to you. At the time the refund is made, a consignment agreement can be concluded for the samples.

A factor to consider is this: Certain direct merchandisers feel that a small initial payment that covers the cost of samples tends to eliminate people who are not sincere about entering your business. Therefore, the few who balk at the small payment are no loss at all.

Your decision about which way to proceed is purely an individual one. Each method has pro's and con's which are inescapable. And either will serve the purpose of helping you reach your fondest income goals.

HOW TO KEEP YOUR PEOPLE WORKING HARDER AND HARDER TO MAKE YOU RICHER AND RICHER

Not long after you start your home merchandising business, you will recognize that one of your most valuable possessions is your organization. In order to keep your people satisfied and to assure the smooth functioning of this powerful machine, you should provide *extra* rewards for good performance.

At the same time, you want to do everything you can to encourage your people to work harder and longer than they ordinarily would. The following three strategies will give you the tools by which this may be accomplished:

1. *Cash Bonuses*

   There are various ways to put extra cash into the pockets of your sub-distributors. "Spiffs" can be paid on certain items in your product line. This is actually a cash bonus over and above the standard commission. You can offer spiffs on products that you bought especially favorably, where the profit structure allows for the additional incentive. Or, if an item is *not* selling well, a spiff will almost always sell it out in record time.

   Each sub-distributor should be made aware of a personal dollar volume quota. This quota gives your salespeople a weekly or monthly production goal and also provides guidelines for your projected merchandise needs. The amount you select as a quota should be totally realistic, yet high enough to give the person something to strive for. When this target is surpassed in a given time period, you can give the sub-distributor a pre-established cash bonus. Needless to say, your people will more often than not be working to make their quotas.

2. *Gift Incentives*

Many successful operators feel that gifts are as meaningful to salespeople as cash. This is especially true if the items you give are of obvious value. You could, in conjunction with your cash bonus program, institute a contest whereby the top producer in your organization wins a TV set, a washing machine, or some other substantial prize (the cost to you will be more than offset by the increased profits generated by the contest). Such events could be conducted as often as each month.

3. *Advancement*

As previously stressed, there are few incentives as potent as promotions to management for most people (but some will shun the opportunity, quite content to be without the added responsibility).

In the early stages of your enterprise, you should set clear parameters for promotion to management and inform every sub-distributor about what it takes to be considered, what the rewards would be, and so forth.

The next step in our program of wealth through direct marketing is a thorough look at the merchandising programs themselves. You'll be amazed at how simple they are to master.

4

HOW PARTY PLAN MERCHANDISING CAN ROCKET YOUR INCOME PRACTICALLY OVERNIGHT

HOW JIM AND LAURA J. KICKED OFF THEIR OWN PARTY PLAN BUSINESS

No two people ever had more reason for being apprehensive about starting a new enterprise. Laura had spent almost all her adult life raising children, and Jim had operated a tow truck for fifteen years—until a physical condition forced him to give it up. Now, without a speck of merchandising experience between them, they were setting out on a party plan operation of their own.

The lack of experience didn't bother Laura in the least. She had attended three home sales parties as a guest and, while impressed with how smoothly and easily it was done, she was sure she could do it as well, or better. At first Jim laughed at the idea of a man and wife partnership, but then realized that he would be playing a vital part in the total effort.

Jim quickly proved to be an exceptionally alert buyer. He attended several business liquidation auctions and made a number of remarkable buys. He also kept an eye out for wholesaler's close-outs and did well there, too. The new company now owned this impressive starting inventory:

- 74 assorted toys and games ranging from 79¢ to $9.95 retail.
- 10 ceramic planters of various colors and size ranging from $1.49 to $7.98 retail.
- 4 musical jewelry boxes, assorted, from $2.98 to $9.95 retail.
- 6 coaster sets, assorted, from $2.98 to $4.95 retail.
- 10 wrought iron and tile trivets, assorted, at $1.29 each.
- Six dozen pieces of glassware including candy dishes, ashtrays, figurines, and others, at $2.98 to $14.95 retail.
- One dozen metal sculpture wall hangings, assorted, at $3.98 to $8.95 retail.
- Two dozen solid brass decor items, assorted, at $2.98 to $19.95 retail.

This product array, plus another ten one-of-a-kind items in various other classifications, made up the beginning display of Jim and Laura's new party plan business.

Laura knew well in advance exactly whom she would invite to the initial showing at their home; in order to virtually assure a good crowd of buyers, she called every neighbor, plus all friends and relatives living within a hundred mile radius. And she asked each one to bring friends. This just about guaranteed a hefty turn-out—and made it a certainty that new faces would accompany the old acquaintances. Each new face was a prime candidate to become a hostess for a future party.

Forty-two people attended the first merchandise showing of Jim and Laura's. By the end of that evening, they had collected $388.26. Three people agreed to hold new showings at their homes, and several others were interested.

The partners disagree on only one point: *The reason for the success of their enterprise.* Jim is convinced it's due to the casual warmth Laura conveys when she phones guests. But Laura insists the response is due to the hostess incentive program Jim devised (each guest can select a free brass or glassware piece just for scheduling a party of her own, plus other rewards if the showing does well).

Jim and Laura are, of course, *both* correct about why their business is successful. And there are these additional reasons why:

1. Acting as a team, Jim and Laura have developed the knack of getting their parties off to a strong start. As soon as the first guests arrive, they both keep the conversation rolling until they are ready to begin showing items.

2. A few minutes after all the guests have arrived, Jim "breaks the ice" and makes the get-together comfortable for everyone by coming up with a hilarious novelty item. After all the guests have a good laugh, the atmosphere is much more relaxed and congenial. At the first party, Jim used a set of candles that couldn't be extinguished by blowing as normal candles are. The item he selects is always in good taste, and is usually very funny.

This couple has used a good measure of *basic common sense* in building a thriving party plan operation. They are prospering simply by *enjoying people*—and by applying time-tested methods (covered in this chapter) that practically guarantee success for them. The same combination would work for just about any other woman or man who enters this remarkable field!

NO MATTER WHO YOU ARE, THE DOOR TO SUCCESS IS OPEN

In discussing party plan merchandising, the term "hostess" is used rather frequently. This may strongly suggest that the field is exclusive to women, but such is definitely *not* the case. While ladies *have* proved to be some of the best operators in the business, many men have made impressive marks, too.

Most women have natural talent in establishing social relationships. They tend to be comfortable talking about their children, community events, and the other topics ladies chat about in the process of building friendships. True, men *can* make the effort to socialize in this way, but most would be quite content to let a female associate handle that aspect of the business.

Therefore, the male merchandiser who wants to tap the huge potential of party plan marketing—but prefers to concentrate his efforts on buying and other equally vital facets of the business— should seriously consider working with a woman. A husband and wife partnership can be ideal. An acquaintance, girlfriend, or relative can work out just as successfully. The basic requirements should be: *the couple must function smoothly as a team, and the man's talents should complement the woman's.*

So party plan offers both the man *and* woman merchandiser tremendous opportunities.

THE ANATOMY OF A THRIVING
PARTY PLAN OPERATION

In the process of creating this book, a sampling of twenty successful direct merchandisers in various American cities were asked this question: "If you were starting your business again, knew what you know now, and could select just one method of merchandising, which would you choose?" Fifteen of the twenty immediately replied that their choice would be the party plan method.

Their reasons for making this selection were varied, but here are a few typical responses: "I don't have to work. My staff does everything except the purchasing." "You start with one party, and it keeps growing and growing without any real effort." "It's probably the most pleasant way people can buy. They're having a good time chatting and socializing, and it's almost like they don't even think about how much they're spending."

The party plan operator simply shows sub-distributors how to recruit hostesses. A host or hostess is any person willing to have a party at her residence in return for a percentage of the total business, or for a pre-arranged gift. The hostess invites friends, neighbors and relatives to the party, so the sub-distributor does nothing except make the initial contact, provide merchandise, and offer to help at the party.

Figure 6 shows the incredible money-making magic of this chain.

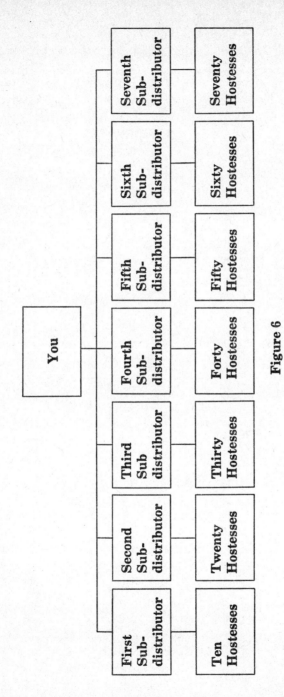

Figure 6

63

IF YOU HAVE SEVEN SUB-DISTRIBUTORS, AND EACH ONE ARRANGES ONLY TEN PARTIES A MONTH, AND EACH PARTY DOES JUST $200 IN GROSS BUSINESS, THAT'S A TOTAL OF $14,000 PER MONTH IN TOTAL VOLUME. IF *YOU* MAKE ONLY 30%, YOUR *PERSONAL PROFIT* FOR THIRTY DAYS OF DOING VERY LITTLE IS A WHOPPING *$4,200!*

Plus, each party gives your sub-distributor *at least* two additional hostesses for future parties, and the future parties provide yet *new* hostesses. The chain builds faster than you can keep up with it!

HERE'S HOW EASY IT IS TO GET STARTED IN THIS EXTRAORDINARY BUSINESS

Before you turn the party plan chain reaction over to your sub-distributor organization, you should gain a working knowledge of how the program functions. The very best way to do this is to give the first few parties yourself.

First, select a day, hour, and place for the event. The day and hour you decide on should be a time when most people are free from other commitments such as work, popular shopping hours, meal times, holidays, and so forth. As a rule, approximately 7:30 p.m. on a weeknight (but excluding Friday nights) is convenient for most people. Also, try to avoid a day and hour that would conflict with extremely popular TV shows.

A word here for readers who may not be able to conveniently hold a home sales party where they live for one reason or another: Since the initial few events are probably the only ones you'll be personally involved with (you'll see why later in this chapter), you can get a friend or neighbor to give the first party by offering that person a gift for his trouble. And this would give you the further advantage of having access to the friend or neighbor's guest list in addition to your own!

Start your preparations by compiling a list of twenty to thirty people. They can be friends, neighbors, relatives, and acquaintances from your place of employment. The more people you invite, the bigger your business will be. Call and invite every person on the list between two and four days before the scheduled showing. If you have extended, say, thirty invitations, you could reasonably expect an actual turnout of fifteen to twenty guests.

On the day of the party and no less than three hours before the established starting time of the showing, set up your merchandise display, organize the refreshments (usually coffee, tea, soft drinks, cookies, and things of that nature).

That's all there is to it! Even *without* knowing the tricks and refinements of party plan merchandising (all described in the following pages), this first event should bring you between $150 and $300 in gross volume, depending on attendance and merchandise selection. But the secrets of America's most experienced operators will *assure* your initial success! Let's explore them.

YOUR CASH AND SUPPLY REQUIREMENTS

1. You'll need order forms that provide a customer copy and an original for your file; standard self-carbon invoices are available in various sizes at most stationery supply stores. This should run no more than three dollars.

2. Any kitchen, dining room or folding aluminum table will make an ideal display area if it's covered with a good, white or light-colored table cloth. This should *not* represent an expense as most households have a suitable table and cloth on-hand.

3. Small adhesive blank stickers or string tags for prices are sold in assortments. Two dollars should supply you with a box large enough for several showings.

4. Six dollars should be more than adequate for refreshments.

5. An important item is name tags for your guests. These introduce the people to one another, and make it easier for you to identify folks quickly, without embarrassing hesitation. One dollar should buy all you need at first.

This is your entire starting supply requirement for your party plan program. The total cost would be in the neighborhood of twelve dollars. As your business gets established, and it becomes important to build an image, you may want to develop custom name tags, order forms, invitations and other forms. Some suggestions are offered later in this chapter.

WHAT SELLS FASTEST AT THE BIGGEST POSSIBLE PROFITS

If there is one cardinal rule to observe when making your merchandise selection, it's that *a wide selection makes sales.* Some of the most successful retail outlets are the ones that offer customers the widest array of products. Thus, the merchandise categories you choose to display at your first showing must be varied.

You *could* base your entire merchandising scheme around a category that's particularly appealing to you personally, but you must realize that such a narrow scope of products would not be as widely popular as would a broad spectrum of general gifts. It would be more advisable to *include* your favorite items, but not let them dominate your total line.

Assuming, then, that general gifts will constitute your line, we can discuss what you'll need initially.

You should display *no less* than forty different items, and more if your budget permits. This starting assortment could include personal and household decor items covering a wide range of tastes and prices. The personal items could be several outstanding jewelry pieces, attractive purses, perfume and cologne sets, and so forth. The decor items can be selected for use in kitchens, living rooms, bathrooms, dens, etc. These products might be decorative statuettes, wall hangings, bookends, planters, or any of countless other accent possibilities.

The actual selections you make when purchasing products for your display can be influenced by factors such as: 1) What type of items are generally in favor with the people you know? 2) What styles are in fashion today? 3) What styles are available from your suppliers? And, 4) which items represent the very best values you can obtain? Every buyer makes mistakes in judgment from time to time, but by carefully evaluating each article when you shop, you can hold errors down to the bare minimum.

Your pricing strategy might follow this suggested pattern:

	Your cost	*Your retail price*
10 products @	$ 1.50 each	$ 3.79 each
10 products @	2.50 each	6.29 each
5 products @	4.00 each	9.95 each
5 products @	5.00 each	12.49 each

	Your cost	*Your retail price*
5 products @	6.00 each	14.95 each
3 products @	8.00 each	19.95 each
2 products @	10.00 each	24.95 each

Your Total Cost $160.00

Total Retail Income $397.50

Each of the ten products you retail at $3.79 would be distinctively different and would thus appeal to almost every conceivable individual preference. Same with the $6.29 items, and so on down the line.

The profit margins shown above are 150%. This is in-line with typical retail margins, and also serves the purpose of giving you adequate cushion for sub-distributor commissions, hostess gifts, and other small expenses. Jewelry can be marked-up 200% or more.

Therefore, your total initial expenditure for supplies and merchandise would be in the area of $172 ($160 for products, $12 for necessary supplies).

HOW TO EXTEND INITIAL INVITATIONS

After your merchandise requirements have been taken care of, the first step is to prepare a guest list. This is simply a roster of all the people you think will attend, up to a total of thirty-five (your goal is to have between fifteen and twenty actually show up). Enter their names and telephone numbers on a sheet of paper. Then, two, three, or four days before the event, sit down and call each one of them.

You: "Hello, Barbara. This is Roberta Smith. Can you come over for an hour or two next Tuesday evening at 7:30?"

Guest: "I should be able to."

You: "Good! I'm having a private showing of gifts I'd like you and a few other friends to see. No obligation, I'd just like to have you here along with anyone else you'd like to bring.

We'll chat and have coffee—and you'll meet
some other people from the neighborhood."
Don't forget to tell every guest they can
bring a friend, or their children (if at
least in their teens). This can rapidly
give you a good crowd of buyers.

Guest: "Fine. I'm looking forward to it. See you Tuesday."

The suggested format is only one of many possible telephone approaches. Use words and phrases comfortable to you as an individual.

The invitation should be extended gently. By all means *do not* insist they come if you encounter resistence. If the person informs you that they probably can't make it, immediately back off and tell them they are welcome if they are free on that evening.

ROOM ARRANGEMENT TIPS THAT MULTIPLY SALES

The next important step for a highly successful party plan operation is to set up your display area and plan the room in which your showing is to take place.

The room you select to use for the party should be the largest in your residence. The living room most often fits this description. The seating must accommodate all the guests you expect (you may have to borrow folding chairs to accomplish this). Your merchandise display should be the *center of attraction.*

Taking a typical rectangular living room as an example, an arrangement that will serve your purpose is to have the products on the table at an extreme end of the room, with the sofas and chairs against the other three walls and angled slightly toward the display. This makes the products easily visible to all without the cranning of necks and leaves the center of the room open for easy movement of the guests.

The products should be arranged on the table neatly, and in groups—all jewelry items together, planters all at one corner, and so on. If products are in boxes, open them. Be sure all items are sparkling clean.

If some of the articles are packed with descriptive labels, be sure these are showing *if* they enhance the items.

When the table surface is considerably larger than the area required to hold your samples, crowd the items into a smaller area, and put order forms or some other relevant papers on the unused part. This makes the selection look more extensive. On the other hand, if the surface is small, crowd as many items in as you can, but do it *neatly*.

Check each product to be sure it carries a price tag, and double check your retail prices.

Finally, just before the guests arrive, turn on every possible light in the room. This gives a bright feeling to the total environment. Turn off radios, phonographs, and TV sets that might interrupt normal conversation.

HOW TO DRAMATIZE PRODUCTS
FOR MAXIMUM SALES PUNCH

Inexpensive, easily obtainable materials can make certain items in your product array look far more valuable than they actually are. Experts claim that these little display tricks can add as much as twenty-five percent to dollar volume.

A high intensity light, or a standard lamp with a powerful bulb, if set up next to or on your display table, will add irresistible highlights to many items. Concentrated light of this kind can bring incredible hues out of even the most ordinary gemstones. Stainless steel gleams like sterling, and brassware can glimmer like valuable heirlooms.

Any fabric shop can supply you with deep, rich velvet material. If this fabric is stretched over a foam rubber piece, and both are stapled into a section of plywood from behind, you have an excellent jewelry display that can be used to enormous advantage at every showing. This expensive looking background makes inexpensive rings, pendants, and watches look many times more costly.

A hand mirror is a must at every showing. Your guests can try on personal decor items and see how they look. A piece that is pretty in the box can become exquisite on the wearer.

TEN SIMPLE STEPS FOR FABULOUSLY
SUCCESSFUL PARTY SALES

The following step-by-step structure is used by many of today's most successful party plan operators. It rarely fails to produce outstanding results.

The overall length of your showing can run from two to four hours. It *must* follow a basic pattern, but at the same time it should be flexible and relaxed. If your guests are enjoying conversation with each other when they first arrive, you wouldn't necessarily rush into the second phase on a rigidly established timetable; let them talk awhile longer and get more comfortable.

Each step is now described. Each includes a time *guideline* that shows approximately how long that particular aspect of a showing normally takes:

1. *Introduction*

   Cordially greet each guest as he or she arrives. Smile and make him feel at home. Print the person's name on a name tag, and immediately introduce him to everyone else in the room (having each guest sign an informal register is invaluable for building a mailing list!).

   As people enter, they will generally form groups where conversation takes place. This is exactly what you want; new friends are being made, and old friendships are being renewed. This stage continues for approximately *twenty minutes.*

2. *Refreshments*

   Serve refreshments now. One person can assist you in pouring coffee and/or soft drinks. This is actually part of the general get-acquainted period, and continues another twenty minutes or so. You're now about *forty minutes* along.

3. *Breaking the Ice*

   The specifics of "game playing" are covered a little later in this chapter. This step "breaks the ice," and gives you control of the group. It's the prelude to the product presentation. An alternative to playing a game is a group joke like the one used by Jim J., described earlier. Either method should take no more than twenty minutes. A total of *one hour* has gone by.

4. *Presenting the Merchandise*

   The product presentation puts you behind the display table giving brief descriptions of your entire line, item by item, group by group. Tell the guests the possible uses of the item; which room it might look best in, what it's made of, and other construction details. Here's how:

"This is a heavy, cast iron tray that looks especially fantastic with Spanish or Modern furnishings. It's used as a candy dish, or makes an ideal ashtray. It will be in your family for generations to come, and it costs only $4.95."

Hold the piece up so everyone in the room can see it clearly, then put it back in your display and go on to the next item. The time your presentation takes depends, of course, on how many items you have to describe. But brief explanations should help keep it down to around twenty minutes, or less. Total elapsed time; *one hour and twenty-five minutes.*

5. *Guest Participation* (For jewelry and other personal decor items)

Modeling is reserved for jewelry and personal decor items. This is actually part of the product presentation, but might add ten minutes more. Here, individual guests are encouraged to try on various pieces to show the other people present how they look in use. This part can be lighthearted since most men and women are self-conscious about strutting around before others. *One hour and thirty minutes* down the road.

6. *Guest Product Inspection*

Immediately after completing your presentation, ask your guests to feel free to personally inspect or try on the items. They'll mill around the table, look at and handle their possible selections, and generally get a close look at all the products on display. This takes about fifteen minutes. *One hour and fifty minutes* have passed.

7. *Personal Attention*

Individual attention should be given to people who have questions about certain items. This is done *while the group is examining the display* (step 6). It helps to be well versed in the nature of each item at this point!

8. *"Closing" Your Sales*

As soon as all questions are answered, you should start writing orders. This will take another ten or fifteen minutes for a total of approximately *two hours.* Don't hesitate to *ask* for orders; any guest who expresses interest in a product should be invited to take it home on a "trial" basis.

9. *Lining Up Future Showings*

Every guest who shows even the barest spark of interest must be approached with your offer to serve as a future hostess. In private conversation in a relatively quiet corner of the room, tell the person that there's a nice gift (or a cash reward if you prefer) in it for him or her, and your assurance of complete cooperation in planning the party. This technique is covered later in detail.

10. *Conclusion*

End the showing by thanking the guests for coming. It's wise for you to offer your help to the hostess in cleaning up.

HOW "GAME PLAYING" MAGICALLY CREATES A BUYING ATMOSPHERE

After your guests have arrived and are busily chatting, you must regain control of the group. If control is *not* achieved, the product presentation will be disorganized. Games are the most effective way to get the attention of every person present.

Some merchandisers strongly believe that small free gifts should be given to every guest in attendance. Each item can cost as little as fifty cents. Distributors and importers carry a number of useful products in this price category. If you decide to use a give-away of this type, the game playing step is the best time to hand them out; everyone who participates in the fun (and also those who do not) gets a give-away gift.

There are scores of truly entertaining games you can use. Here are two possibilities:

In *FARM FUN,* give each guest a card with the name of an animal written on it. When every guest has a card, you tell a story that eventually introduces each animal. As soon as a particular creature is mentioned, the guest holding that card must immediately simulate the sound of that animal.

The story can be as simple as this: "Farmer Smith woke up early one day to the crowing of his rooster (a "cockadoodledoo" from the guest holding the card marked "rooster"). He had breakfast and went out to feed the hungry pigs (an "oink" from the audience—and almost certainly laughter from the other guests). The barn was his next stop. Mr. Smith headed for Elsie because he knew she'd be ready to give him lots of milk. Sure enough, there was his favorite cow (a "moo" from that guest)." You might want to give an extra little bonus gift to the guest who does the best or funniest animal sound.

You might try this variation occasionally: Give *everyone* present a card with "cow" written on it. Thus, when the first animal you name is cow, it's met with a chorus of "moos!"

MEMORY MADNESS is a longtime favorite. It's both entertaining and it helps people remember the names of other guests. With the guests seated in a big circle around the room, the person to your right starts by selecting an animal that rhymes with his or her name; such as "Jake the Snake," "Mary the Dromedary" or "Pam the Ram." Then, the next guest repeats the name of the first person, and makes one up for herself. The third guest in the circle repeats the first two, makes up a name, and on it goes—all the way around the room. By the time the twentieth guest has a turn, there's a bit of remembering to do!

AFTER THE FIRST PARTY, YOU SIMPLY SIT BACK AND RAKE-IN THE CASH PROFITS

When you personally take this first home merchandising showing from its inception through every step, you will gain enough background to train sub-distributors. As soon as they are trained, they can run the business *for* you. The initial party probably revealed that as many as five guests would be willing to hold showings at their homes. This is the beginning of a chain reaction that grows like wildfire; these guests, plus your sub-distributors, are the nucleus of your own party plan merchandising empire.

You would arrange a meeting between yourself, the first new hostess, and the sub-distributor to whom you are turning over the operation. A party date would be arranged at this meeting. After you spend a little time training your sub-distributor in the ten steps covered earlier, *it's the last time you ever have to get directly involved in organizing sales parties unless you want to!*

The new hostess knows an entirely *new* set of people she can invite to her party. In this group, there are several *new* hostesses who agree to invite yet *new* people. *Your* major responsibility is to keep the products flowing, and new sub-distributors coming so your business can keep expanding. It becomes what *must* be the easiest way in the world to get rich!

The key to $36,000 a year, and much more, in party plan merchandising, is *the effective recruitment of new hostesses.* Here's how to ensure that objective:

HOSTESS INCENTIVES . . . THE SMART WAY TO ACCELERATE YOUR SUCCESS

There are two ways to convert guests into new hostesses:

1. *Offer them a choice of any gift in your product line at no cost.*

   This is especially compelling to a guest who is admiring one of your best watches, or an elegant cookware set, and simply can't afford it. You might see her eyeing it fondly, but not making a move to buy it. After you positively determine that she can't possibly fit it into her budget, you tell her it's free if she invites her friends to a party at her home. It'll get the job done almost every time. And the cost to you will be only around ten to fifteen dollars (your cost for the item).

2. *Or, offer them a cash incentive*

   Certain guests will respond more positively to an offer of hard dollars. The best way to do this is on the basis of a percentage of the total sales volume resulting from the showing he or she holds. The advantage of this system is that you will get the active participation of the host or hostess in making the party a success; the bigger the final total sales are, the bigger the commission will be.

   You can work on five to ten percent of the total party sales volume. Thus, a modest $200 showing would pay the hostess as much as $20 for the night. And it's entirely conceivable that the commission could go as high as $30 or $40. Not bad for having your friends over for a few hours!

Whether you give a gift or cash to your hostess, the reward should be conspicuously delivered at the end of the showing.

When the guests see how well it can pay to have a party, they may be influenced to ask you for details. *But don't wait for guests to volunteer!* Your recruiting effort should begin the moment you start to take orders. *Every person* you talk to individually should be offered the opportunity to have a party of his own. Then, at the end of the evening, ask the guests once again, as a group, if any more of them are interested. Those who are interested can stay a few minutes later and work out preliminary details with you or your sub-distributor.

TEN HOURS PER WEEK
YIELDS $18,500 YEARLY INCOME FOR MILDRED A.

Mildred A. makes $9,450 a year working forty hours per week in a factory. Her party plan business produces an additional *$18,500 a year in profits and takes only ten hours a week, or less, of her spare time.* Her total income is $27,950!

Mildred intends to devote full-time to her party plan business starting in a few months. When she does, she estimates her earnings will reach *$40,000 to $50,000 a year!*

"I never realized that making money could be so easy and fun. One day my daughter returned home from a trip to Arizona loaded down with Indian style jewelry. She had spent her last hundred dollars on a box full of those things, and I was ready to hit the ceiling! At that moment, I didn't realize the importance of what she had done."

Mildred and her daughter each took a couple of pieces to wear as part of their wardrobe. In one week the jewelry had attracted so much attention, they decided to make a business out of it. Almost everyone who saw the jewelry wanted to buy it. So Mildred invited some people from the factory where she worked to come over and see the entire collection at her residence. Her daughter did the same thing with friends from school. They sold out in three days and made back the hundred dollars . . . plus $288 in profits!

They both made a trip back to Arizona as quickly as they could, and reinvested their profits in the most beautiful costume rings, bracelets, pendants, and pins they could locate. Now, they sell such a huge volume of merchandise, the suppliers come to *them.* And so do prospective sub-distributors; the two party plan operators now have nine people busy arranging new showings.

Mildred has instructed her sub-distributors to offer willing hostesses a selection of any jewelry piece they desire up to $40 retail—plus a bonus if the party grosses over $200.

"My daughter and I personally hold two showings every week. We could let our organization do all the work, but we still love being involved," reports Mildred. "We've become kind of famous, and people come from miles away to buy from us or our new hostesses. Several of our sub-distributors are earning around $8,000 a year. All of them have hostesses who give parties at every opportunity. They find it the best and cheapest way to get the jewelry items they want, that they've never been able to afford!"

THE ADVANTAGES OF PRE-PACKING PRODUCT ASSORTMENTS FOR YOUR SUB-DISTRIBUTORS

There is no better program to operate in terms of merchandise management than party plan. There is absolutely *no need* for your sub-distributors to purchase merchandise! All you need is a wide assortment of product samples that they can pick up from you and take to the showing they have arranged. Orders are taken from the samples at the party, and the assortment is returned to you the next day.

This method requires that you have sources of supply which can provide customer orders quickly and accurately; guests would prefer to have their selections delivered within one week, and they are justifiably fussy about getting items that are *identical* to the samples they saw at the showing.

As your organization grows, and the number of parties each week increases, your array of samples will have to grow accordingly. You may very well encounter situations where two or three sub-distributors need products to show during the same evening! But when you have an extensive inventory of sample products, it permits each sub-distributor to vary his display from showing to showing. He will never run the risk of having the line look stale; it will be ever-changing and dynamic.

If you use this system, be certain to prepare an inventory list of all the items your sub-distributors take to showings, and always remind them that the assortments must be returned to you promptly and intact (in rare instances, a guest will not be able to wait for a factory-fresh item to be ordered and delivered, and will

want to buy the sample right out of the display. If you wish, you
can authorize your sub-distributors to make sales like these when
absolutely necessary).

ESTABLISHING AN IMAGE
FOR YOUR RAPIDLY GROWING NEW BUSINESS

"Image" is very definitely an overworked word in business,
and one that is used incorrectly more often than not. Image is *not*
the exclusive domain of corporate giants. It's of vital concern to
even the smallest operators.

When consumers hear a company name over a period of
months or years, they associate it with a certain category of
products, a certain level of performance, and with quality — or
the lack of it. Part of the image-building process depends on the
way you and your sub-distributors conduct your day to day transactions. If you are cordial, helpful, and truthful, your business
will gradually come to mean all these favorable things to the
public.

If your products give the consumer fair value for the dollar,
that becomes known to people. And when you stand in back of the
items you market, it's one more big point in your favor.

But a serious mistake made by many business people is the
quality of their image *in print*. They may do the best job they can
in every other respect, but they fail miserably by producing sloppy business cards, order forms, and other literature seen by the
impressionable consumer. The good work they do is to no avail
because they are frequently judged by the way they look on paper.

When your enterprise is just getting started, you can make do
with standard forms purchased in stationery stores. But as things
get rolling, you would be wise to have *professionals* do your
designing and printing. This list shows the elements you'll want
as soon as you can afford them:

- *Business Cards* (Every guest should receive one. You may
  get telephone orders *after* showings)
- *Customer Order Forms* (Should be in duplicate, and simple enough for a child to complete without assistance. They
  should be imprinted with your logo and business name and
  address)

- *Party Invitation and Confirmation* (Used when you can't reach people by telephone. Can also serve to confirm invitations that are made by phone)
- *Hostess Instruction Sheet* (Sub-distributors give it to each future host and hostess. It describes everything they must do to prepare for showing merchandise in their home. It also might include blank spaces where a guest list can be entered)

Many good printers can get help in graphics at little or no cost to you above the printing itself. This can include a logo design, type styles, ink colors, layout, and even paper selection. You'll be proud of the results, and your customers will be impressed.

DOING BIG BUSINESS WITH ORGANIZATIONS AND CLUBS

Several of the most prosperous merchandisers in America do nothing else but help various groups raise funds for worthy causes through party plan sales. It's a gold mine just waiting to be worked.

Church and youth groups, women's clubs, charitable organizations, and community improvement associations, to name just a few, all need cash to make their programs work. They hold bazaars, carnivals, auctions, and numerous other activities for fund raising purposes. Home merchandise sales are a natural for them.

The organization would invite its entire membership to see your merchandise display. You or your sub-distributor would work out a system that gave the group a slice of the profits. Thus, they make badly needed money at little or no cost to them.

Your local classified telephone directory and Chamber of Commerce might provide a complete list of such organizations in your area. They could bring you important dollars, while you help people who are less fortunate.

ARLENE P. TELLS ABOUT A GIGANTIC CASH OFFER FOR HER NEW PARTY PLAN BUSINESS

She was laid off her clerical job in August, started her own party plan merchandising business in September, and *refused to sell it for $32,000 the following October!*

When Arlene P. started marketing her own cosmetics line in August, the last thing on her mind was making a big business out of it. She merely intended to make enough money to cover living expenses until she could find another job like the one she had recently lost. But it "got out of control," according to this beginning business operator. "Women were calling me day and night asking me to display my line of fragrances for this group and that group. I was going at top speed seven days a week until I lined up three sub-distributors to help me."

Here's how it got started: Several days after she lost her job, Arlene heard about a small local perfume manufacturer who was willing to produce private label merchandise; the firm would apply any identification the customer desired on its standard perfumes, colognes, and other beauty items. Arlene visited the company and liked what she saw. She was able to talk them into consigning her a relatively small quantity of items. Then she had attractive labels put on the bottles, and the rest happened naturally, without any real effort.

One of Arlene's neighbors agreed to hold the first home showing of the new perfume line. This woman invited almost everyone she knew in the area, and thirty-three women showed up. The party grossed $377 in just three hours . . . *and most of it was profit!* From that start, Arlene set up three more parties within the following week, and every one of them did as much business or more than the first one did. It hasn't stopped growing since!

In September, Arlene received a long distance call from a man who said he represented a large national merchandising company. He said they had looked into adding a fragrances division to their operation, and felt hers might work out well. He asked Arlene to spend several days discussing the acquisition, and plane tickets reached her by return mail. She met with the owners of the firm. They offered the young woman cash and stock in the company that totaled $32,000 . . . plus an employment contract that would give her the position of vice president of marketing in their new cosmetics division!

"Maybe I'm crazy, but I refused the offer," reports Arlene. "I'll make at least $40,000 this year without really trying very hard. Plus I'm doing what I like to do—and I'm my own boss. Besides, I really don't think I've scratched the surface. The poten-

tial for personal income could very well be in the hundreds of
thousands of dollars!"

An interesting development took place in Arlene's extraordinary career shortly after she made the decision to remain in her
own business. She embarked in direct sales along with party plan,
and almost immediately added big volume to her already soaring
income. The next chapter describes exactly how this fantastic
merchandising program works.

5

HOW DIRECT SALES CAN BRING YOU THE SAME RICHES IT BROUGHT TO AMERICA'S RETAILING GIANTS

ONE OF THE OLDEST FORTUNE-MAKING BUSINESSES IN THIS COUNTRY

In 1838, Joseph Seligman learned that farmers living in distant rural areas were forced to make arduous wagon journeys to the markets in town. The recent immigrant astutely reasoned that if he were to bring the goods directly to their doors, these people would gladly buy from him.

With his modest savings, Seligman bought a variety of merchandise. With a pack on his back, he set out for the farmlands. He and other peddlers of the day frequently slept in open fields, or in the comparative luxury of barns if they were fortunate enough to be offered chores to do in return for a night of shelter.

Joseph's theory was: "Sell anything that can be bought cheaply, sold quickly at a little profit, small enough to place inside a pack, and light enough to carry." By doing exactly that, Seligman became one of the first known people to build a financial empire through direct sales.

During the more than one hundred years since those days, a countless number of fortunes have been made through offering merchandise directly to consumers in their homes. It is one of the few major industries in the world that has remained essentially unchanged over the years; today, an individual would find it almost as simple to begin in business as Joseph Seligman did in 1838. And, equally important, it can be accomplished now with the same kind of small cash investment required a century ago.

HOW SIMPLE IT IS TO GET STARTED IN A BIG, BIG WAY

If you decide to start a direct sales business in the morning, you can be operating in full swing by the same afternoon! There is no easier field to enter and few that can be started as quickly— with as much promise of success. It consists merely of packing an assortment of product samples in a carrying case and showing these items to all the people who reside in a pre-planned marketing area—simplicity itself.

Transactions are on a cash basis, and customer selections are usually delivered at the time of purchase. Thus, your cash outlay for products multiplies rapidly, your inventory turns over fast, and you have minimal record keeping.

The first step is acquiring merchandise. Because your stock will be traveling with you, try to select items that are compact and relatively lightweight. That would rule out large pottery pieces, bulky cookware sets, and so forth. The most advantageous items are small, individually boxed gifts that give you economy of space and ease of handling. Of utmost importance is having an interesting, widely diverse selection; you'll want to appeal to the greatest possible cross-section of consumer preference, and that demands *variety*. Fastest selling product categories are covered later in this chapter.

Selection of a sample case should be made *after* your product line is finalized. This, of course, enables you to more closely pinpoint your precise needs. As a general rule, the case should be of a durable, lightweight material, yet spacious enough to hold *at least* fifteen items or more.

Next, you'll need order forms. These are available at stationery stores in various standard formats. Be sure to get one that provides duplicate copies of each order you take—one copy for the customer, one for your file. Finally, business cards: Most local printers can suggest attractive layouts using your personal or company name and address. Cards serve the vital purpose of giving your business an image of permanency.

That's how easy it is. You now have everything you need to begin what should turn out to be a highly profitable, rapidly growing direct sales business!

A FRANK LOOK AT START-UP COSTS
In addition to its high success probabilities, the direct sales field offers you the opportunity for a strong start in your own business at a low, low initial investment. For the sake of example, let's assume you select your starting product inventory based on four price categories. The prices shown are at *your cost:*

a. 10 different items at $2 each $20
b. 5 different items at $4 each 20
c. 3 different items at $6 each 18
d. 2 different items at $8 each 16
   Total initial product outlay $74

This assortment will give you a solid base of impulse-appeal retail prices, yet includes several items in the fine gift category. An expenditure of $74 at your cost should yield approximately $185 in gross sales, or more; a profit of $111. This is based on a 150% markup. Jewelry can be marked-up 200%, or more.

The above formula can, and probably will, vary. Its final shape depends on your product preferences and what you feel will sell best in your particular area.

Your expense for a carrying case should be well under $25. You may be fortunate enough to already own a case of some type that would be suitable for use until your business can buy you a new one. If so, you can invest the savings in additional products or back-up stock, if you wish.

Order forms and business cards should not exceed $13 in total costs. Therefore, your total initial start-up costs are as follows:

1. Beginning inventory of 20 products $74
2. Carrying case 25
3. Order Forms and business cards 13
   Total *$112*

As your new business grows and prospers, you'll want additional supplies such as a personalized rubber stamp, custom imprinted letterheads and envelopes, etc. But the above list represents your *total* starting investment in a fantastic opportunity!

KEN F. WAS FLOORED WHEN HIS $200 INVESTMENT ZOOMED TO $6,200 IN JUST FOUR MONTHS

"Orders seem to come from everywhere. It's like the holiday buying season 365 days per year! I can do business every day I feel like making calls. On one day I'll never forget, I had over $200 in profit . . . and that was only a few days after I started operating!"

Ken got started when he was laid off his regular job. He had no background in any other field, and not enough income or savings to fall back on. He was suddenly faced with the necessity of finding something he could handle that would produce dollars *fast*.

After some research, Ken learned that big money was being made in various direct-to-consumer fields. After further investigation, he picked direct sales on a door-to-door basis. He knew it would take nerve to knock on doors—and he had never sold anything before—but he was determined to make it work.

"I invested practically my last funds, $200, in gifts I felt would be popular. On my first day out, two people gave me sizable orders and paid cash. I knew instantly that I was on my way to a fortune!

"The most surprising thing about it is the fact that I never have to 'sell'; it's just a matter of asking them if they'd like to see my gift selection, and the rest happens automatically. They see what they like . . . and they buy!"

Ken reports that in only four months, his initial $200 product investment has grown to $6,200. Profits reach $2,000 per month. He added this: "There's nothing in the world like being your own boss. You pick when you want to work, and how much you want to make. There is absolutely no limit."

But even more exciting than the $24,000 income Ken expects to make in his first year of operation, is this: He has been approached by two solidly established, well capitalized merchandising companies that want to acquire his young business. One of them made a substantial cash offer for his customer list and inventory, the other also offered to buy him out, and they want to make him national vice-president of marketing at a starting salary of $30,000 per year, *plus* bonuses, an expense account, and stock options. As much as Ken enjoys his new freedom and prosperity, he is seriously considering the latter proposition. He figures it's worth more than $50,000 per year.

But if Ken decides to retain his enterprise and keep it growing, it's reasonable to expect that the offers will get bigger, better and more numerous as time goes on. It's entirely conceivable that he could create an operation within just a few years that would command offers in the *million dollar* class. Ken has mixed emotions about selling out now because he is sure that this will, indeed, happen.

GETTING THE MOST OUT OF YOUR MARKETING AREA

Even if you have been a long time resident of the area you plan to work, chances are you really don't know it as thoroughly as you could. In direct sales, *every* home and apartment holds the promise of a big volume, high-profit order; each business firm might be a source of enormous business for you over the months and years.

Therefore, you should set about the task of defining your marketing area and learning every nook and cranny within it. One excellent way to do this is to obtain a current, highly detailed city map, one that shows every street clearly and accurately.

First, give some thought to assigning yourself reasonable boundaries. Remember, you're the boss, and you are free to take as large a territory as you wish, wherever you want it to be. But keep this in mind; you should be able to call on *every* resident and business firm in your marketing area no less than once each three to four weeks. Spreading yourself too thin will make proper follow-up impossible. On the other hand, an operating zone of reasonable proportions can be a joy to manage and should arrive at financial maturity much faster.

As soon as you have defined your area, try to find out where population concentrations are. Large apartment complexes can yield a tremendous amount of business, as can medium to large business firms. Single family homes should not be overlooked; nobody, regardless of how long he has been in direct sales, can predict where the big orders will come from.

Now, divide your marketing area into segments. You might try to make the divisions in two or three block sections that can be color-coded directly on the map by felt tip marker. If you thoroughly cover one segment at a time, you'll be assured of getting the most out of your area.

THE LAW OF AVERAGES *ASSURES* FINANCIAL SUCCESS IN THE GIANT DIRECT SALES FIELD

One of the top earning direct sales operators related this intriguing story:

"It was my first day out and I was petrified. I started on the first floor of a twenty-unit apartment building. I was almost relieved when the tenant in the first apartment didn't answer. Then, the second and third weren't home, either. The fourth one was there, but said through the door he wasn't interested. I don't mind telling you how discouraged I was beginning to feel, but I went to the next door.

"A woman answered and invited me in after my introduction. After I nervously showed several items, she excused herself and made a few fast phone calls asking neighborhood friends to come over. In a short time, I was answering questions for a group of women. Within forty minutes, I had $132 in orders!

"Since that day, I don't know the meaning of the word "discouragement." If a string of successive calls gets me nowhere, I'm *sure* a big one is just around the corner. The percentage works for me *every time!*"

If you make the calls, the business *will come*; it's a game of numbers, pure and simple. In fact, after you have worked your area for awhile, you'll be able to arrive at a highly accurate formula that shows how many visits it takes you to get an order!

Some direct merchandisers boast ratios as low as one sale for every four calls; others claim it takes them ten visits per order. In any case, you can take great comfort in knowing that the law of averages is solidly on your side. Now, here's an example of how averages may be used to attain your income goal:

If the particular merchandise selection you are showing yields an *average* profit per order of, say, $18 and if you are *averaging* seven visits per order—you *know* you'll make $54 per day by visiting approximately twenty-one prospects. The resulting $324 per week in profits gives you $16,848 per year.

Therefore, to reach $36,000 per year, you would need another $19,000 in profits. If you recruited two people to work other parts of your city, each would need only about $180 in weekly profits to get you there. A chart later in this chapter illustrates potential income through salespeople in yet another way.

The point is, you can use the law of averages to attain almost any income level you want: When you know the size of your average profit . . . how many visits it takes to get an order . . . how much business the typical salesperson you recruit will bring you . . . you can tailor your direct sales organization to produce almost exactly the kind of earnings you desire, whether it's $36,000, or much more!

EIGHT STEPS TO A FOOLPROOF PRESENTATION

An organized presentation will make your day-to-day contacts with potential customers a pleasure. You will never grope for words, or be unprepared if unusual situations arise.

Your presentation should be a step-by-step procedure that stays on a definite track from the time you knock on the customer's door to the time you depart for your next call. Although you may in time evolve an approach that fits your personal style, here's a basic technique you might use in the meantime:

1. Ring, don't knock, if the home or apartment has a doorbell. If not, rap firmly, but no more than three times. Wait 30 seconds before knocking again if there is no answer. Knock more firmly the second time. If there is still no answer, proceed to your next call.

2. When your prospective customer answers the door, immediately take a short step back, away from the door. This is important in eliminating any pressure the customer might feel if you were too close to the entrance.

3. If the people are in the middle of a meal, entertaining guests, or are otherwise involved, excuse yourself and tell them you will return at a more convenient time.

4. Under any other normal circumstances, smile, promptly introduce yourself, and describe the purpose of your visit. Customers will invariably receive you more warmly if you are straightforward and brief.

5. If the customer expresses an interest in seeing your products, and invites you in, spread *all* your items on a surface such as a tabletop. On the other hand, if the customer tells you she is not interested, be gracious and leave. By all means do *not* try to pressure your way into a residence.

6. Remain on your feet unless invited to sit down. Try not to rush, but at the same time always remain businesslike. It is wise to politely refuse all offers of refreshments on initial visits. This becomes a matter of judgment after you establish the person as a customer.

7. If the prospect does not express specific item preferences, you can proceed to show each of your products, giving a short description of each one.

8. As soon as you have taken the order, thank the customer and leave.

NO "SELLING" NECESSARY! LOW-PRESSURE CAN GET CONSISTENTLY BIG DOLLAR VOLUME AND PROFITS

The era of the back-slapping supersalesman has vanished. There was a time when people responded to slick, fast-talking hucksters. But as the general public became better educated and more sophisticated, high-pressure selling came to be regarded as offensive.

In this day and age, any individual who attempts to use these old methods in a direct-to-consumer business would quit in frustration. The buying public is very likely to laugh this operator out of business.

Unfortunately, the word "sales" still carries a stigma from the old days. This causes many people to avoid rich careers that bear little resemblance to what they were years ago. The fact is, today's successful salesperson reaches wealth by being likeable, honest, and by providing good personal service.

If a customer says "no," that's that. If the reason for the negative response is because the item is the wrong color, then you must offer to obtain the *correct* color. Forcing the prospect to take unsuitable merchandise might earn you a fast profit . . . but it will almost always destroy the likelihood of future repeat orders and the valuable referrals that come from satisfied customers.

Low-pressure in direct sales is effective due to the situation prevailing in typical retail stores. The average customer must contend with self-service when making a purchase. There are usually no store employees available for answering questions about products on display. The direct sales specialist can therefore provide outstanding service simply by being informative and helpful.

One of the other principle keys to growth in direct sales is permanency. When neighborhood residents see you for the first time, they may hold back on a purchase merely because they are not sure if you'll be around if service is ever needed later. In these cases, the follow-up visit will get the order. A low-pressure approach will serve the purpose of leaving the door open for your all-important second call. In contrast, if the customer has an unpleasant experience as a result of high-pressure, there will be *no* chance for a follow-up.

When you believe in what you are doing, that feeling will be conveyed to your potential customer. It does *not* take a carefully rehearsed act to transfer enthusiasm to customers. When you carry the pride of being the owner of your own company, and you have personally selected your product line with great care, most people will *feel* your sincerity!

WHAT TO SAY AND HOW TO SAY IT
FOR DRAMATIC RESULTS

In the eight basic steps of the presentation, there are three areas that require dialogue on your part. These are: the Introduction, the Product Description, and the Conclusion.

The words you actually use can have a bearing on how quickly you reach success. As with the approach, this will evolve from what you find personally comfortable and natural. You may also discover that certain phrases you test from time to time get better results than those you tried during previous calls.

This is *not* to say that phrases should be memorized! By all means avoid that. The intent of the following examples are to demonstrate the *kinds* of impact that should be conveyed to customers; you may find that you never say the exact same words twice, but the meaning of the overall statement will always be essentially identical.

1. *The Introduction:* "Hello. My name is Robert Smith of Smith's gifts. We have a beautiful line of home and personal decor items I think you'll find interesting. Would you like a quick look at them?"

This accomplished the fundamentals of immediately divulging who you are, the name of your company (if appropriate), what you deal in, the purpose of your visit, and the fact that you intend to be brief. It is done all in one, short sentence. The delivery should be pleasant, sincere, and accompanied by a smile. Again, the precise words can vary depending on how you feel about them.

2. *The Product Description:* "I personally select domestic products, and imports from all over the world. We can assure you of exceptionally good values on attractive, quality merchandise. Here's a good example; this solid brass urn is fine enough to become a family heirloom. It makes a magnificent planter, or a striking dining table centerpiece . . ."

Quality and value were stressed before beginning the merchandise descriptions. When the first item was shown, basic details about its construction and uses were given. Whenever practical, let the prospect actually handle the item. Watch customer responses carefully; if a spark of interest is detected, place the item on a nearby shelf or table where it might appear to be part of the existing decor. If it's a jewelry item, let the prospect wear it. If no interest is observed, proceed to the next item. When fitting, use glamor words like "magnificent," "striking," "elegant," "superb," and so forth.

3. *The Conclusion:* In some instances, customers will not come right out and say "I want that watch" or "Here's a check, please give me the cutlery set." Thus, you should politely ask for the order at the completion of every presentation. If you were carefully watching the prospect's reactions to each item, you undoubtedly detected that one or more generated some interest. If so, say something like this after you have completed the descriptions:

"I would suggest the teak salt and pepper set; it complements your other kitchen decor and gives that counter a needed accent. Can we set it aside for you while you try on the ring again?"

Return to the points of interest and try to conclude sales, as illustrated above. If there were no expressions of interest, ask the prospect what her particular needs are. You can always obtain special requests when you do your purchasing.

HOW JIM S. STARTED IN BUSINESS IN THE MORNING AND COUNTED HIS FIRST IMPRESSIVE PROFITS THAT SAME AFTERNOON

"After several months of unemployment, I was flat broke, down to my last ten dollars and some odd cents. For me, survival was now a matter of a place to sleep and enough food for the next few days.

"I was as desperate as it's possible to be. Then, I remembered that several years ago a friend of mine had done very well selling direct to consumers. I figured if he could do it, why not me? There was no time to waste, so I charged head first into the direct sales business. I knew nothing at all about it, but I was willing to learn.

"I visited a merchandise distributor downtown. After looking at the few items I could afford, I decided on a carton of one dozen suede ladies change purses at $9.60. They were colorful, of decent quality, and I felt women would like the photo windows, credit card holders, and other features they had.

"I jumped into my car and headed toward the first residential neigborhood in the area. I made my first call at about 11:00 a.m. By 1:30 p.m. I was sold out. My $9.60 had suddenly grown to over $21. Each 80 cent purse brought me an easy $1.79 retail and probably could have brought $2.98 just as easily!"

Jim reinvested his profits, and more than doubled them again the next day. As time passed, his product line expanded and his business continued to thrive. Within only six months from the day he desperately purchased one dozen purses, he had parlayed his last $10 bill into a robust firm that was putting *$175 per day* in his bank account!

Within three weeks of his first day in business, Jim had recruited and trained four people to sell for him. Since then, he has added an average of one additional salesperson each two weeks. At the six month point, his entire state was covered by this growing organization!

Jim projects *personal profits in excess of $100,000* during his next full year of operation . . . all from one dozen purses!

HOW TO QUICKLY BLANKET YOUR COMMUNITY WITH SALESPEOPLE EAGER TO MAKE YOU A MILLIONAIRE

As well as you may ultimately do in personally working your own marketing area, it will still be only a small step toward the kind of prosperity you can eventually reach.

If your own efforts produce clear profits of $40 to $60 per day, harder work will not increase it enough to build significant wealth. There just isn't enough time in each day. Therefore, if you are content with an income of $10,000 to $15,000 per year, it might be best for you to continue your enterprise as a one person operation. But if you have your sights on $36,000 per year or more, you should turn to the incredible power of the 30 million opportunity seekers who are eager to make extra money for themselves, and a fortune for you.

Through selective recruiting of opportunity seekers, you can rapidly accomplish astounding expansion in an amazingly short time. As described in Chapter 3, it would be necessary for you to *personally* make sales calls for several weeks after starting your business, or just long enough for you to develop an organized program you can give to your new representatives. They, in turn, will do all the footwork for you.

The easiest people to recruit are those you call on. You can be sure that a surprisingly large percentage of the men and women in your area need extra money. Many of them desperately need part-time jobs, but don't know where to turn. And some would surely consider your direct sales business a perfect full-time opportunity.

Here's how simple it is to get them started distributing your merchandise: During the course of conversation with a prospect or established customer, you can say something like this: "I just can't keep up with the business we're doing. If you know of anyone who wants to make big money for a few hours work each day, please let me know."

The prospective direct sales recruit may not take the bait right then and there. Sometimes pride can prevent a commitment; he may want to maintain the illusion that everything is under control financially. Or, he or she may have to check with a husband or wife before even considering undertaking a new career. Therefore, if you observe some interest, but there is no further discussion on the subject, call back several days later and say something like this:

"Remember I mentioned needing assistance in my business? The more I think about it, the more I feel *you* would fit in. Would an extra $25 to $50 per day interest you?"

This would rarely fail to get you a new representative *if* the individual is a likely candidate to begin with.

You should be prepared to immediately show the new recruit exactly how to proceed. These points are recommended:

1. Assign a specific marketing area with defined boundaries. It should be easily accessible to the recruit.
2. Consign product samples and order forms. Business cards can either be purchased by the new representative or supplied by you.
3. The price structure you plan should allow the new representative respectable profit margins. For example, if your cost on an item is $2 and you decide to retail it at $4.98, you can charge your representative $3 for the item. That gives you a 50% profit and your new salesperson more than 65%.
4. Familiarize the recruit with the approach and dialogue you have successfully used. You might also accompany your new representative on calls during the first day out.

AFTER A FEW WEEKS, THIS PHENOMENAL BUSINESS CAN VIRTUALLY OPERATE AND GROW BY ITSELF

Let's take some *conservative* figures to see what direct sales growth can do for your bank account:

If you decide to take it easy and personally make only $30 per day in profits working 5 days each week, that's $7,800 per year just from your efforts.

Now, hold on to your hat; Figure 7 shows how your income can skyrocket when you add representatives. If each recruit buys $20 per day in merchandise from you (to do that, he would need only about $38 in gross sales based on 150% mark-up), your daily profit from each would be $6.50, or $32.50 per 5 day week.

Number of recruits	Your profits for one week	Your profits for one year	Your annual earnings with personal sales of $7,800
1	$ 32.50	$ 1,690	$ 9,490
3	$ 97.50	$ 5,070	$12,870
5	$162.50	$ 8,450	$16,250
8	$260.00	$13,520	$21,320
15	$487.50	$25,350	$33,150
20	$650.00	$33,800	$41,600
30	$975.00	$50,700	$58,500

Figure 7

You can now see how your time will come to be devoted to the growing task of supplying merchandise to your expanding sales organization, not to mention the continuing responsibilities of uncovering new product sources. If you follow the next step, the biggest headache in this business—the job of keeping a heavy flow of recruits coming—is automatically taken care of. Here's how to do it:

After you have successfully obtained 5 to 10 representatives, you should start the process of grooming one of the outstanding ones for a supervisory position. This would entail the responsibility of overseeing the other representatives, and would also include the job of attracting brand new recruits. For this, your supervisor would get a small percentage of the total business done by every person he or she recruited, in addition to the usual profits from personal sales which should continue normally.

An alternate plan, and one that is perhaps more effective, is to offer your representatives a valuable gift for any new recruits they refer to you. If the incentive is of value, it would assure you of an ever-growing organization, the key to riches in this field.

When your direct sales business is at a stage where you have representatives covering your entire city, you'll be well on the way to bigger income than you ever imagined possible. And if you set up the mechanism for getting new representatives as described above, it will practically run itself. You will be free to take care of the vital demands of a thriving company.

HOW ANNE R. ESTABLISHED A BOOMING DIRECT SALES OPERATION MORE POPULAR THAN MOST RETAIL STORES

"Frankly, I was getting more and more upset by the experiences I was having in neighborhood stores", Anne R. told me. "My friends were also complaining. There were times I stood and waited twenty minutes for help. When someone finally *did* arrive, he acted like he was doing me a favor. And to make matters worse, the clerks usually couldn't answer the simplest questions about products I wanted to buy!

"Another thing was the condition of items in many stores. It would by typical to buy a nice gift, take the sealed box home, open it, and discover that the item looked nothing like the sample I had selected from. Then, to add insult to injury, I'd have a battle with the store manager getting it exchanged. These problems all stemmed from a lack of personal attention.

"These things made me furious", she continued. "I'm a grandmother, but I decided to take action by starting my own gift business for the folks in my neighborhood. I resolved to give people the kind of quality and service they are entitled to.

"I do business with several importers. They let me inspect new products under a magnifying glass if I want to. When I'm with customers, I'll let them take just as much time as they need to be sure the product is right. If they have questions, I can tell them everything there is to know about the item. If problems of any kind come up, I'll take care of them, no questions asked.

"One day, one of my lady friends invited me to bring my samples to her place of work. She was a secretary for a company employing around fifty women. During lunch hour, I took $120 in orders and made eight appointments for home presentations! Since that day, calling on business firms has been very much a part of my activities."

Anne R. reports spending $300 every week for products. At moderate profit margins, she makes in the area of $300 per week, part-time. But equally as important, she's having the time of her life. Her customers simply will not buy gifts anywhere else.

USE THESE METHODS AND YOU JUST
CAN'T MISS BIG, FAST MONEY!

The direct sales success stories you have seen are just a sprinkling of *thousands* that occur every year in every corner of America. Prosperity in this method of merchandising is *not* a matter of speculation; it's an absolute certainty IF YOU FOLLOW THE PROCEDURES PROVIDED IN THESE PAGES!

The expensive, risky testing and experimentation has been done for you over long years of trial and error by others. The foolproof methods described have been refined and perfected to the ultimate degree.

Most beginners encounter problems when they attempt to depart from the accepted formula; they gradually introduce changes to the proven steps. These small variations alter the character of an enterprise, thus diluting its strength and impact. $36,000 PER YEAR IN DIRECT SALES IS WITHIN THE GRASP OF VIRTUALLY ANY AVERAGE ADULT WHO IS WILLING TO APPLY BUSINESS GUIDELINES THAT *WORK:*

The initial start-up phase of your business should be kept as simple as possible. By using the minimum number of forms, as explained earlier, you'll be free to develop your area . . . where the profits are. You will not be saddled with the task of spending unproductive hours behind a desk keeping elaborate records.

Your beginning merchandise selection should be confined to a *basic assortment of known best-selling products.* That will serve the vital purpose of quickly increasing your capital, enabling you to reinvest your money: $74 becomes $185 which grows to $370 that turns into $740. Then before you realize it, you have $1,480, $2,960, and it multiplies steadily and rapidly. In six months it could become $40,000, even $70,000!

The law of averages is an unchanging fact of nature. If you *know* that each day of moderate effort in your marketing area produces *personally* generated profits of only $40; and the people you have recruited only give you another $75; that's a total of $115 per day. You *know*, then, that six days per week will produce

$35,880 in profits for you during the year. It's not only completely realistic to set that kind of income as your goal, it's actually *conservative* in this remarkable business!

Planning to *get the most out of your marketing area* is one more easy-to-do step toward assuring big income. By becoming known, trusted, and respected among the consumers you deal with, you'll most likely *pass* your original income dreams by a substantial margin.

And no less important is the eight-step presentation and the ways suggested to present items to your customers and prospects. By being consistent, polite, and low-pressure, you'll rapidly become polished and professional. New buyers will be added to your list in ever growing numbers. Referrals will begin to come on a daily basis. It provides yet *another* reason why $36,000 per year, or much more, isn't magic!

Therefore, you can join the biggest direct sales earners in the world by doing exactly what *they* have done to reach prosperity.

Our fast-moving way of life has brought one more merchandising method into a position of extreme importance. Because people are on-the-go as never before, it pays to go out and find them; this maximizes your total effort if a large percentage of potential buyers are not home during daytime hours. The way to do this is through mobile showroom merchandising a discussion of which follows.

6

HOW MOBILE SHOWROOM SALES LET YOU TAP ENORMOUS IMPULSE-APPEAL PROFITS

THIS INCREDIBLE IDEA TOOK THE DIRECT MERCHANDISING FIELD BY STORM

While retail stores maintain an endless vigil waiting for the buying urge to strike their customers, mobile showroom merchandisers are out with the people, sweeping in the bucks.

As fast as lightening, this remarkable operator appears, instantly produces a dazzling display of products, and as quickly as orders are written up and delivered, is off to some promising new market blocks or miles away. Customers are delighted to be spared the hassle of battling shopping center crowds, and the indifferent service that prevails in the average store.

There is no marketer in creation who can react more rapidly to seasonal needs and local demands; the mobile merchandiser appears on sunny beaches with boxes of sunglasses, at rainswept intersections with colorful umbrellas, and at midwinter football games with battery-operated handwarmers.

In this business, you're the closest possible thing to the wagon merchant of the old frontier. But your vehicle can be anything from a hatchback sedan to a big panel truck. You have unbounded freedom, unbelievable flexibility, and astounding wealth potential.

You can operate a mobile showroom in conjunction with any of the other programs described in this book; party plan or direct sales can easily be operated evenings while you are prospering out on the streets during the day in your vehicle, and mail order fits hand-in-glove by virtue of your rapidly growing customer list.

ENJOY THE SUNSHINE WHILE THE CASH POURS IN

For those who love the open air, there are few other fields that offer the combination of being outside and the potential of making big, big money. You slide behind the wheel in the morning, and you are never confined inside for the rest of the day.

While you are enjoying the delights of nature, you can easily take in up to $500 a day, and more. At a normal profit margin of 100%, you'd need only $300 a day to make *$39,000 per year*! Here's how easy it actually is to do $300 in one average day (this was, in fact, an average day for Tommy G., one of the top mobile merchandisers in the business):

8:30 a.m.   *Sales*

Parked van in front of a large factory
in plain view of workers entering gate .... $ 32.23

9:50 a.m.

Stopped at a large office building
in time to show products to people
on break 30.00

10:40 a.m.

Made stops at the fringes of several
busy shopping areas 58.60

12:10 p.m.

Parked and displayed merchandise on a
well travelled street in an industrial
area to catch workers going to lunch 115.09

2:00 p.m.

Drove to a high school area and
showed merchandise to kids on their
way home 26.77

4:30 p.m.

Back to a factory area to see more
people heading home 44.40

Total Gross Volume for
the Day $307.09

Tommy reports, "The day was a breeze. Everything about it was a pleasure; the weather was beautiful, the people friendly and agreeable, it was perfect!" But the outstanding thing about it was the neat *$150 profit* for several hours "work."

If Tommy G. had "hustled," had really run from stop to stop, and had not taken a leisurely lunch hour, he could have dramatically increased the day's take. But he's making phenomenal money and is thoroughly enjoying every moment of life to the fullest.

TAKE YOUR DEPARTMENT STORE-ON-WHEELS WHEREVER YOU WANT TO GO, WHENEVER YOU FEEL LIKE GOING

The key to riches in mobile merchandising is your ability to be where the business is at exactly the right moment. Your territory is your neighborhood, your city, your county, or your state—wherever you feel like going on a given day.

People are ready to buy anywhere, at any time. So anyplace you decide to go, you'll do business. On some days, you'll get many small orders from many brief stops. On other days, a certain street or office building will be magic; people will stream to your display in a never-ending procession. You'll sit there for hours and do an entire day's business in one spot.

The following day, you may feel like going fishing. So you pack your gear and head for the lake. When you arrive there, you find dozens of other people who have the same idea. You set out your merchandise display, drop your line in the water, and do a good day's volume while you relax.

As time goes on, you get to know the places that are likely to be good stops—and the best times to make those stops. With this knowledge, you can do some pre-planning. As you pre-plan, your mobile merchandising business becomes tremendously efficient; you find you can get twice the amount of dollar volume in half the time.

Before long, you will see that $36,000 a year, and more, can be achieved in just three or four days per week!

ALMOST *ANY* VEHICLE MAKES AN IDEAL
ROLLING SHOPPING CENTER

Of course, the more selection you can carry, the better your business is likely to be—but virtually any kind of car or truck can quickly be adapted for successful mobile merchandising operations. The first requirement is display space, the second is storage area for back-up stock on especially popular items.

In this method of merchandising, you want to *deliver* the item to your customer at the moment of purchase. You wouldn't take orders from samples as you might do in party plan. Therefore, if you expect to sell, say, twenty-five sets of Christmas tree lights during a day in December, you must somehow be able to carry that stock with you. In a small sedan, this would present an obvious challenge. In any camper, mini bus, station wagon, or similar vehicle, it's a cinch.

The typical family sedan, if it has an unusually large trunk (for your display), and a spacious back seat (for back-up stock), can suffice.

The very best mobile shopping centers are panel trucks with fully enclosed cargo areas. In these vehicles, pegboard racks can easily be rigged up to hold many items. If large enough, customers can come aboard to make their selections. Boxes of inventory can be stored neatly toward the driver's end of the display area.

Whatever you drive at the present time can be used for the time being (except perhaps a motorcycle or a roadster). If your operation grows and prospers as quickly as it should, your *next* vehicle purchase can be planned with an expanded mobile merchandising business in mind.

HOW TO MOST EFFECTIVELY DISPLAY
YOUR MOBILE SHOWROOM PRODUCTS

Pegboard sections are the way to go in displaying items for mobile merchandising. Hooks and brackets that are especially designed for use with pegboard panels are available at many large hardware stores and office supply companies.

When items come packaged on cards, the cards can be punched to hang on the pegboard from hooks intended for that purpose. When packed in boxes, shelves can be fitted to the sections. Larger items can remain on the floor of your trunk or cargo area, as the case may be.

If you own a van, truck, station wagon, camper, or mini bus, the pegboard panels can be designed to stand along the interior of the display area inside the vehicle. Items hanging from the pegboard by hooks won't go anywhere until you or a customer removes them. Products on shelves, however, can be kept in place by fishnet stretched over the front of the shelves and secured top and bottom. This method keeps them from tumbling down when you drive over bumpy streets or navigate sharp turns.

If you have a vehicle that isn't large enough to accommodate standing panels like the ones described above, you can have portable pegboard display racks made at very reasonable cost. These would have detachable bases. They can be kept in the back seat, or on the top of your vehicle, and can quickly be set up *outside* when you make a stop. This, in addition to keeping your trunk wide open revealing yet more merchandise, attracts as much attention as a van brimming with items.

Portable panels can be in the area of three to five feet tall, and three or four feet wide. This size can hold an amazingly large number of items on hooks and shelves combined.

Also, don't overlook the possibility of carrying a folding aluminum table, if you can fit it in. This can be set up outside and loaded with products in a matter of minutes, and makes an exciting splash to passers-by.

HOW BILL O. POCKETED OVER $2,000
FOR EVERY 400 MILES OF ENJOYABLE TRAVEL

Bill O. and his wife Marge are teachers. During summer vacation, they decided to drive their camper across the western U.S. to see as many of the spectacular sights as they possibly could in the space of two months.

After they described these plans to Tom D., a friend of theirs, he suggested they sell products from the camper as they passed through towns on the way west. Tom said it would not only make the trip more interesting, but would finance the entire vacation.

So the couple took $275 of their precious vacation funds and made a purchase from an importer who carried products of every description, available at prices well below prevailing retail levels.

The week before they were scheduled to leave, Bill put together two pegboard display racks and bases. It took him less than four hours of work and cost just over $25 including all the necessary hardware.

Full of apprehension, Bill and Marge left on a Monday morning and drove until lunchtime. They stopped for sandwiches in a small town. As soon as the two vacationers finished eating, they set up the display racks for a little while to see what would happen. The teachers took in $168 *in less than 30 minutes!*

From that time on, the couple displayed almost every time they stopped. And each stop was fantastically profitable; when the two months were over, the two teachers still had their original $700 vacation savings, *plus over $5,000 in clear profit!* That works out to $2,000 in gross sales for every 400 miles of travel. And this was a *vacation!*

Bill is making plans to become a full-time direct merchandiser. He's sure he can make way over $50,000 a year, and enjoy the scenery 365 days a year!

WHERE TO FIND CROWDS OF BUYERS
WHO FLOCK TO MAKE PURCHASES FROM
MOBILE SHOWROOMS

A major element to consider when seeking the best location in which to make mobile sales is population concentration; where are large numbers of people to be found who would be apt to buy from your display?

The second aspect to think about is this: What products can you show those people that would get immediate acceptance?

The answers are deceptively simple. Here are just a few to give you an idea as to how simple they actually are:

1. You can find scores of women around office buildings and shopping centers. They will buy panty hose, cosmetics, toys for their children and grandchildren, jewelry, or any other items that ladies buy in any other type of store.

2. You'll find hundreds of teenagers at the beach during summer vacation or around high schools during the school year. They would buy records, clothing items that are in vogue, novelty auto accessories, or hundreds of other products that are traditional best-sellers to this big, wealthy market.

3. Sports fans will, of course, be found around high school, college and professional sports stadiums at game time in the thousands. If the weather is cold, they'll buy items designed to keep them warm, and vice versa during summer.

4. People at recreation areas on camping trips will buy pocket knives, fishing accessories, flashlights, batteries, candles, radios, playing cards, games, and an endless list of other products that can be useful in that particular environment.

So there's no magic in becoming a smart merchandiser. It takes only a little thought and imagination about the next place to go with your mobile showroom and some advance planning in obtaining the types of items that would be appropriate for the location you choose to visit.

Planning as basic as this will assure you of tremendous customer interest wherever you stop and will keep your profits soaring!

VERA C. TELLS HOW ACTION AND COLOR DRAMATICALLY INCREASED HER BUSINESS

Mrs. Vera C. has been a mobile showroom merchandiser for three years. She had seen the enormous potential in marketing to consumers by truck after working aboard a food catering vehicle for a year; "The people working at the businesses I serviced were always asking me for non-food items, so I finally resigned, loaded my station wagon with merchandise, and that was that.

"I made $10,000 during the first six months. It was okay, but nothing to rave about. I had expected much more. I tried everything I could think of: different items, different prices, different areas, but nothing seemed to put me over the hump.

"One day a customer said something to me that really rang my bell. He gave me a nice order. Then, as he was leaving, he told me he had almost driven right past my display on his way home from work. He said that my station wagon looked like a stalled vehicle pulled off to the side of the street, but that he happened to get a glimpse of the items and came over.

"The next day I had two enormous signs made out of window shade material, one for each end of the car so *nobody* would miss me. They read LOWEST PRICES ON TOYS, GIFTS, AND NOVELTIES in big, red letters against a bright yellow background. They roll up and store in a small area in a few seconds. I also bought pennants in all different colors that I can fly from the antenna. The boldest step was a portable yellow rotating light. That *really* turns a few heads!

"Results came immediately," Vera says. "My records show a twenty-five percent increase in the number of customers I got during my second six months in business. But the incredible figure was my dollar volume; it jumped over *fifty percent*! In my second six months, I made almost $16,000 in profits. My second full year in business gave me an income of just over $36,000!

"The big breakthrough came when I set my first agent up in business. A man I got to know asked me if he could distribute my merchandise in a neighboring town. We worked out a buying arrangement, and now I make an additional $8,000 just on *his* business. That comes to $44,000 yearly, and it's still growing! I plan to add at least one more sub-distributor every two months!"

THE FIRST STEP TOWARD A MOBILE MERCHANDISING SUB-DISTRIBUTOR OPERATION IS ROUTE PLANNING

While you certainly gain big chunks of easy income through the recruitment of sub-distributors who buy merchandise from you and operate their own mobile showrooms, you also lose some of the freedom of movement you enjoyed when you did it all on your own. Territories should be exclusive and protected. If not, you and your agents will constantly be crossing paths and duplicating efforts.

The ideal situation is one like Vera C.'s; she lived in an area where there were many small towns, and it was simple for her to assign an *entire town* to a new sub-distributor. But in a large city, some thought must be given to the division of territories.

If you plan to continue the operation of *your own* mobile showroom, you want to preserve enough population concentration for continuing personal profits. On the other hand, your sub-distributor must have every chance to get off to a good start, and he or she should also have the freedom to rove freely in search of business.

Therefore, the area you designate for a sub-distributor must be substantial in this type of merchandising, but must take into consideration *your own* mobile operations, plus the possibility of *future* expansion with the addition of yet other sub-distributors.

A fact well worth mentioning at this point is that the territories you assign for one type of merchandising have nothing whatever to do with the territories assigned for others. For example, a specific slice of real estate that is set aside for a sub-distributor operating a mobile showroom can also be worked by different sub-distributors engaged in party plan, direct sales, and mail order. The area is protected *only* to the extent that you would not permit another mobile merchandiser to work it.

IMPORTANT NOTICE TO READERS:

You are strongly advised to obtain all required state and city permits before beginning merchandising operations. There might be severe penalties in the event you are apprehended while doing business without the necessary licenses.

Since there are no uniform requirements from city to city or state to state, it is impossible to advise you in this book what your specific procedure should be in conducting operations legally. The best course of action is to inquire at local city halls immediately upon arriving at a particular locale. Find out these two important things:

1. What permits are needed for operations within the city itself.
2. What permits are needed for operation of a home merchandising business within the state.

It's well worth the little extra time to get this out of the way as soon as you can since these permits are usually valid for a long period of time and are of nominal cost.

Conducting a direct mail program in conjunction with any of the other merchandising methods does *not* require state or city permits. You simply need to comply with Postal Service mailing regulations, even if you send mailings all over the country. Read on to find out how to make a fortune in direct mail.

7

GET YOUR SHARE OF $50 BILLION IN YEARLY MAIL ORDER SALES

WHY THE VAST MAIL ORDER BUSINESS IS A NATURAL FOR YOU, THE PROFESSIONAL MERCHANDISER

$50 billion a year in sales puts mail order in the big leagues of American industry. It stands at the side of such giants as automobile manufacturing, food wholesaling, oil, and others.

It seems that a week doesn't pass without a story about some new mail order millionaire. Some of the people who reach wealth in this dynamic industry are totally inexperienced; they make it on sheer luck. But most often, a good idea, courage, and sound planning produce these overnight riches. Success in mail order is practically a certainty *if* solid business principals are applied . . . like the ones described in the following chapter. There is no need to rely on the vagaries of luck if you are a successful direct-to-consumer merchandiser, and you are willing to practice proven methods.

In the process of operating a party plan, direct sales, or mobile merchandising business of your own, you are perfectly situated to get your fair share of the enormous wealth that is spent every day for goods and services through the mail. Here are some of the reasons why:

1. You are closer to the consumer than almost any other successful mail order operator, and you will therefore be able to determine the direction of buying trends that are taking shape in the market.

2. You will have access to the most treasured commodity in this industry, strong mailing lists.

3. You will often be the first to uncover those certain magic items that skyrocket to mail order popularity by virtue of your close contact with importers and other suppliers.

4. You will be in the enviable position of being able to test market new items, thus proving their consumer acceptance before investing in mail order promotion.

Remember, this incredibly rich business was *built* by merchandisers like you!

GET A BUNDLE OF MONEY
DELIVERED TO YOUR DOORSTEP EVERY WORKING DAY

A few of the rewards that can come to you as a result of building a strong mail order business are as follows:

1. Compared to any other method of selling goods to consumers, mail order profits are virtually automatic. There is no contact with customers to speak of; you can have reasonable assurance that right after you send out a mailing, the checks and money orders will begin to arrive. You don't have to leave the comfort of your home to make it happen!

2. The *repeat* business can be dynamite. As your business matures, the percentage of return on your mailings in-

creases. And, as a general rule, the orders get bigger and come more frequently as time goes on.

3. The income you can make in mail order will bear no relationship at all to the time you are required to devote to the operation of your business. As little as five hours a week can produce $300, $500, $1,000 each week in profits, or even much more!

There is no thrill greater than opening your mail box and finding it jammed full of envelopes addressed to you, each one containing money . . . and an order for your merchandise. This unbelievable experience can occur *every working day of every week*. It does for many people in this field.

If you are patient, and follow these steps to the letter, it will almost surely happen for *you!*

HOW TO GET STARTED
AND EFFECTIVELY ELIMINATE RISK

The methods proposed in this chapter are designed to give you sure-fire ways to establish a thriving mail order business that functions *hand in hand* with one of the other direct-to-consumer operations—party plan, direct sales, or mobile merchandising.

We are interested only in getting you quickly established in the booming mail order field so you can start producing important income that will grow and keep growing. Equally important, these methods will virtually *eliminate risk*. This business is laid out for you *scientifically, not* as a winner-take-all gamble the way it is so often presented, unfortunately, by certain so-called experts.

If there is, indeed, one simple success formula that must be observed in prospering through mail order, this is it:

YOUR MAIL ORDER BUSINESS MUST BE BUILT BY USING A CUSTOMER BASE THAT *YOU* HAVE PERSONALLY ESTABLISHED THROUGH OPERATION OF A DIRECT-TO-CONSUMER MARKETING METHOD.

This means that in the beginning stages of your mail order operation, you will do business *only with individuals who have made purchases from you at some time in the past.*

112 GET YOUR SHARE OF $50 BILLION

THE BEST MAILING LIST AVAILABLE ANYWHERE, AT ANY PRICE

From the day you start doing business in party plan, direct sales, or mobile showroom merchandising, *you must be absolutely sure you get the name, address, city, state, and zip code of every single person who makes a purchase from you, regardless of how large or small that purchase may have been.*

At the same time, you must also get the names and addresses of every customer your *sub-distributors* do business with.

This procedure would rapidly give you a mailing list that could not be equaled at any price from any other known source. It would very likely yield a customer response of at least four percent, and very possibly as high as seven percent, on every mailing you send out. In contrast, lists you rent or purchase from brokers are unknown quantities at best. They may be used by operators of all kinds offering items of all descriptions. It would be an understatement to say that the people on such lists are subjected to a barrage of mail. Your chances of being lost in the shuffle are far too great. That's why customer response on rented or purchased lists runs only one or two percent as a rule.

Your customers . . . the people who have made purchases from you or your agents . . . are the people who know and trust you. When they see your offer in their mail, they will remember you, and they will respond *far* more often than they would to companies unknown to them. But when *you* mail to a rented list, then *you* are the unknown company, and your mailing is generally discarded, unread.

So, by concentrating on getting orders from your customer list, you are laying down an excellent foundation for the building of a powerful mail order business, and you are proceeding in the safest possible way from the standpoint of financial risk.

BEWARE OF MAIL ORDER RIPOFF SCHEMES: HOW TO SPOT THEM

Perhaps the best way to illustrate the *wrong approach* to mail order is to describe one of the most blatantly exploitive rackets taking place in America today.

The endless stories we hear about mail order fortunes being made—some of them true, some partly true—have created a tremendous interest in this field. The result is that thousands of beginners hopeful of making personal fortunes have fallen victim to certain firms who prosper by promising big, easy mail order money to these people.

This group of companies usually offers the aspiring mail order operator pre-printed mailing pieces, merchandise, instruction manuals and occasionally mailing lists. In a few instances, the new business person is required to pay the firm a membership fee for the privilege of buying those supplies!

The overwhelming majority of people who get involved with these firms are destined to failure for the following reasons:

1. Pre-printed mailing pieces might be full-color merchandise catalogs or relatively simple black and white flyers. In any case, they are printed by these companies in enormous quantities to hold down costs, then sold to individual mail order operators at large profits.

    The cost is one thing, but the biggest problem is that many, many consumers see the mailing piece two or three different times, from different sources every time. It's entirely possible for a given residence to receive three identical catalogs in one day, with a different company name rubber stamped on each catalog cover! If this doesn't permanently destroy the image of a new mail order company, nothing will!

2. The merchandise offered by these firms is usually stale and shoddy. The items can be found in practically every novelty shop, drug store, and discount house. The products are flashy, but cheap—and certainly not conducive to customer satisfaction.

    To make matters worse, the beginner is paying the firm very near retail prices for merchandise that must carry at least a four-fold profit in order to be profitable through mail order (a $1.00 item should be offered at $3.98, or more).

3. Such firms either recommend a local mailing list broker, or take it upon themselves to rent the starting operator lists. These will run the beginner $20 to $30 per thousand names, and will rarely yield more than a two percent return, as mentioned earlier.

    As if that were not bad enough, many of these lists are not properly maintained, and as many as thirty to forty percent of the names and addresses might no longer be deliverable. If the mailing is sent via third class bulk rate, the operator might never find out that most of the people on the list never even see the offer! (In using third class bulk rate mail, the only way you would receive the corrected addresses of undeliverables would be to pay 18¢ extra for each returned mailer).

Therefore, you must *avoid* companies who advertise easy, overnight fortunes in mail order using catalogs and merchandise they peddle to you at huge profits. They exploit people who are inexperienced in this field. These firms are the *only* ones who prosper in such programs—and they do it at the expense of those who don't know any better.

These are precisely the problems you will avoid by using the methods prescribed in this book.

TESTING: THE PROFESSIONAL WAY TO BUILD A MAIL ORDER EMPIRE OF YOUR OWN

If the biggest, most successful mail order corporations in the world test market products before investing serious money in them, why wouldn't you? You have, after all, ready access to thousands of consumers who will express opinions about any product you choose to show them. They will either approve of it, or reject it. If necessary, such a study can be completed in a matter of days.

As you visit various suppliers in the course of your buying activities, you will occasionally come across new products that stand far above the others in terms of mail order appeal. Such items might possess these basic attributes:

1. *They have mass market appeal, but are not widely exposed on store shelves or in other mail order catalogs.*

   This can be achieved by purchasing goods produced by small manufacturers who turn out unique items, and don't have the facilities to flood the market. Also, *stay away* from highly popular products that have been around awhile (one of the most common errors made by new mail order operators is to buy things they see everywhere). As often as possible, buy a *newly introduced* item so *you* can be the one to make money on it . . . *before* it's peddled by everyone at every street corner.

Avoid radios, small appliances, and any other product category that is commonly promoted by mass merchandisers at low prices in newspaper ads and TV commercials. These are usually low profit items, and you'll never be able to compete favorably. Try to locate products that are used in currently popular areas. For example, if plants and planting are enjoying a surge in popularity, you might do well to select items related to that field. If tennis is dominating the sports scene, try to acquire some kind of tennis accessory, and so forth.

2. *They should be attractive, and could be effectively illustrated or photographed (some items are especially difficult to portray on a printed page, and are thus poor mail order selections).*

   A fine porcelain, brass, or crystal bud vase might be a perfect mail order gift possibility, but can it be shown effectively on a catalog page? Yes, but it takes excellent photography or illustration to get the point across. A heavy gauge vinyl swimming pool cover may be extremely popular through direct mail, but first you must find a way to illustrate it. A picture of it all rolled up certainly won't help you sell them - but a picture of a swimming pool being protected during a blizzard certainly would.

3. *They can be offered at a popular price, but still give you at least a four-fold profit.*

   Popular brand merchandise is often ignored by experienced mail order operators; it's simply too easy for the consumer to compare with identical items on local store shelves. Your potential customer will buy unknown makes almost as quickly as big name brands, so why make it too easy to check your prices? In a mail order ad, an off-brand can be glamorized to look as good or better than a top brand - and will thus be able to stand a higher retail price to give you the profit you need.

4. *They should be compact and lightweight in order to keep mailing costs in line, and make handling reasonably convenient.*

   A tropical plant would undoubtedly make a very good mail order seller, but how do you ship a heavy, fragile pot full of dirt and delicate foliage at nominal cost? You can't. A large wooden children's playhouse could very well be in strong demand, but how can it be transported without doubling the retail price? It's a problem. Take a hard look at each possibility in order to determine its ease of handling and shipping.

If these qualifications are satisfied, you might have a potential winner. But before you invest in photography, printing, and postage, you should buy a sufficient number of these items to give your sub-distributors. They should be instructed to carefully watch customer reaction when this particular product is shown.

If the item sells briskly, its mail order possibilities would be established. But sales figures alone sometimes don't tell the entire story. Your sub-distributors should be listening for consumer comments that might provide some clues that would strengthen your marketing effort. For example, the ultimate buyer might think of uses for an item that may never have occurred to you *or* the manufacturer.

You'll seldom make mistakes when you test as thoroughly as this. Almost every item you select for mail order promotion will become a profit producer, and each one will enhance the reputation of your company.

TWO MAIL ORDER OPERATORS DESCRIBE HOW TESTING PROVIDES THE KEY TO BIG MAILING PROFITS

Annette C. has a friend in the retail jewelry business. He had purchased an assortment of solid gold choker type necklaces and offered them to her as a way to make a few extra dollars selling them to friends. Annette bought the group from the jeweler at a few dollars over his cost.

She showed the assortment to people she knew from her college classes, and several of the styles turned out to be exceptionally strong sellers. On the basis of this limited success, the young woman made the decision to move quickly into mail order with the gold pieces. She was confident that by exposing the group through mailings to large numbers of men and women working in office buildings near her home, a fortune could be made, much more than would be possible by showing the items to individuals (which time didn't permit because of her studies). Annette also knew that success would arrive more rapidly by promoting *only those necklace styles that had already been enthusiastically purchased by her first customers.*

Each necklace Annette selected *did* turn out to be a hot seller, as her initial experience indicated it would be. Therefore, during the first stages of her efforts, she didn't waste *a cent* on promoting products that were not proven! This strategy made her a clear $7,270 in her first three months in business!

Dwight K. built a direct sales organization of ten people covering three states. His product line was based on handmade wood household accessories such as small shelves, decorative cannister sets, knife racks, and similar items. He was anxious to expand his sales through mailings, but was at a loss in selecting a small group of specials from his vast assortment of styles.

The answer came to him almost accidently: While Dwight was reordering merchandise from his suppliers one day, he noticed that in one region, eight wood pieces outsold the rest of his line by a margin of nearly three to one. If these were photographed and put into a mailing piece, why wouldn't they receive the same acceptance as they had on a direct sales basis?

Dwight prepared a circular showing this group, and sent it to a list of 6,000 people consisting of old customers and new prospects in middle class neighborhoods in five small cities. Despite expectations of a break-even on his first try at mail order, Dwight netted $1,105 on this promotion! He feels it's just the beginning of bigger things to come . . . thanks to his foolproof method of picking winners by watching the results of his direct sales operation!

WHAT TO MAIL
FOR THE BIGGEST CASH RETURNS

For the sake of example, let's say you've been operating a party plan business for four months, and you have three sub-distributors working other areas. Through your combined efforts, your mailing list totals over 2,000 names—each a satisfied customer who has made a purchase before.

Over a period of several weeks, you have come across two products that promise to be outstanding mail order sellers, and a market test supports your enthusiasm. You feel the next step is a major mail promotion that would be launched with a mailing to your customer list. If this mailing is successful, you would proceed to step three; a media advertising program.

You prepare a simple one page circular with this headline:

FOR　　OUR　　CUSTOMERS　　ONLY . . . TWO
FANTASTIC　VALUES　FROM　*(Name of your
company)*

Beneath the headline, you include a subhead that reads:

*Specially Purchased in Limited Quantities—This
Spectacular Offer Good for* 10 DAYS ONLY!

Large drawings or photographs of the items should be included, plus descriptive copy for each that would provide information on the size of the item, its uses, construction, price, and so forth (Figure 8).

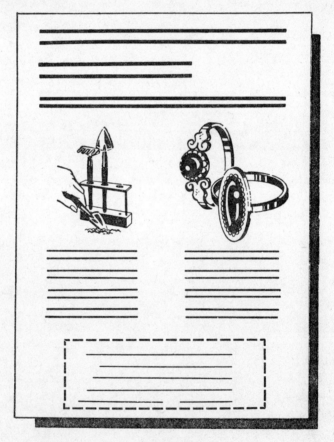

Figure 8
This layout indicates the general look of the
mailer described

The last element in the circular is a small order form that the customer can cut out and mail to you. It includes a line for state tax, if applicable (Figure 9).

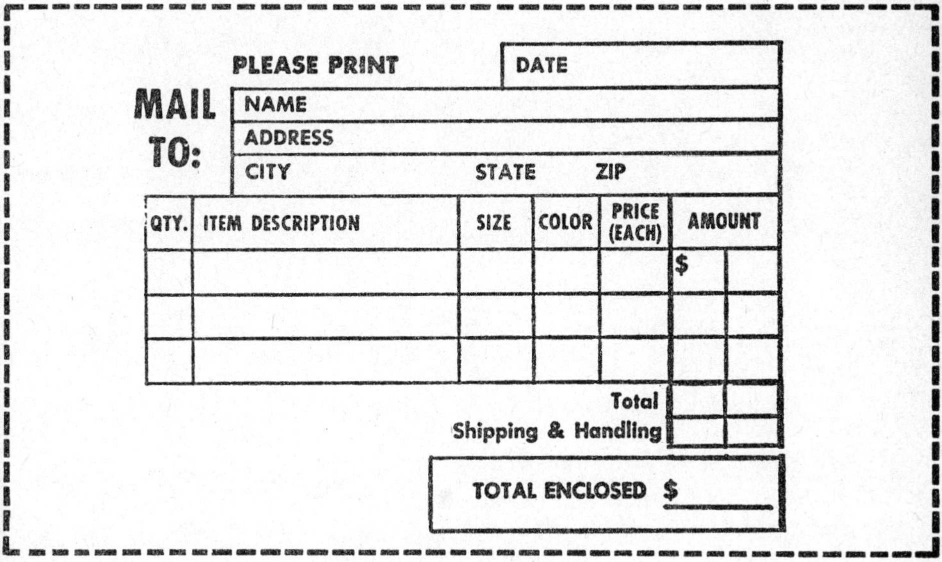

QTY.	ITEM DESCRIPTION	SIZE	COLOR	PRICE (EACH)	AMOUNT

PLEASE PRINT — DATE — MAIL TO: NAME, ADDRESS, CITY STATE ZIP — Total — Shipping & Handling — TOTAL ENCLOSED $

Figure 9

You may want to charge your mail order customers for postage and handling. If so, a schedule of charges must also be included. It might look like this:

If your order is . . .   *Please add . . .*

up to $4.99 .... $1.00
$5.00 to $9.99 .... 1.50
$10.00 to $19.99 .... 1.75
$20.00 or more 2.25

The figures you actually use would be based on prevailing postage and mailing material costs, plus handling expenses as you calculate them. If you do *not* incorporate such a schedule, postage and handling must be included in your retail prices. Most experts agree that the separate schedule is preferable because it allows lower selling prices.

Now your mailers are folded and inserted in standard envelopes. Reply envelopes can be pre-printed with your address and a first class reply permit (this allows the mailing of an order at no postage cost to your customer. *You* pay the postage when the letter is delivered to you. These permits are available at no cost from the Postal Service). Or, you can omit the permit and require your customers to affix stamps of their own (the permit method will probably get a little bigger response since it makes ordering easier. It may be well worth the extra cost to you). In either case, this envelope is inserted with the circular, and your mailing is ready to go.

HOW WALLY K. BECAME INDEPENDENTLY WEALTHY IN MAIL ORDER IN ONLY SIX MONTHS

Wally K. is one of those people who attained quick success by following proven merchandising strategies. Here's a brief chronological rundown of the events that propelled him to wealth:

April: He started a direct sales and mobile showroom merchandising business. By the end of the month he had recruited eight sub-distributors and was doing big business in every corner of his state.

May: By midmonth, he had collected a group of four items that he felt were sure mail order smash hits (a polyester sleeping bag at $11.98 retail; a wrought iron-look wall hanging weather station including barometer and thermometer at $7.49 retail; a five-function hand calculator at $5.88 retail, and a 1000 watt hair blower/styler at $13.98 retail). Wally exposed this family of items to his sub-distributors. They held customer previews on the products in their respective territories and reported excellent buyer acceptance.

June: Wally prepared a flyer showing the four products (each one fortunately made an excellent presentation on the printed page), and sent out a mailing to 5,000 customers. He received a six percent return (300 orders) amounting to over $6,000 in business. Wally immediately had ads prepared and placed in eight strong mail order oriented national magazines and two syndicated newspaper magazine supplements. He also increased retails on the four products by 15% to cover advertising costs.

September: During August and September, Wally received *$34,770 in orders* for the product group (the hand calculator surpassed sales expectations. The sleeping bag was second, the blower third, and the weather station failed to come up to sales projections). In September, he sold his direct sales enterprise for $20,500 and retained sole ownership of the mail order business.

In six months, this merchandising beginner netted a total of *$31,878* and set the stage for future mail order promotions that could *triple* that sum. He placed a blockbuster media campaign with a portion of his profits that he expected would produce gross revenues of almost *$90,000!* And that, Wally felt, was merely the first step!

MEDIA ADVERTISING: SOME GOOD AND BAD POINTS

So the perfect mail order business—the one that holds the total potential for generating enormous profits—is the one that utilizes both mailings to existing customers *and* media advertising. The mailings, in addition to producing important business, also give further proof of product acceptance.

Because of the high cost of media advertising, such further proof is *absolutely necessary.* The amateur who buys untested items from a distributor and proceeds to purchase expensive advertising space in magazines might as well put a match to his cash. But it happens every day.

Magazines and newspapers are treacherously dangerous places for naive advertisers, but at the same time *they are precisely where the millionaires are made.* Therefore, if you can enter this dynamic marketplace with products that are absolutely certain winners, the odds for success are excellent.

But proven products are not the entire answer. There are still two extremely important things you must do before you charge into national advertising with your items. They are:

1. You must select the best publications for your purposes.
2. You must come up with the strongest possible ads in the smallest amount of space.

FINDING THOSE CERTAIN PUBLICATIONS THAT HOLD THE KEY TO SPECTACULAR MAIL ORDER FORTUNES

There is no shortcut to zeroing in on a group of, say, three or four magazines that will do the job for you in mail order. While it *is* desirable, practical, and possible to considerably narrow down the field just by looking at publications, the fine tuning requires—that's right—more testing.

Any magazine, syndicated supplement, or tabloid newspaper that carries a large number of mail order ads is in the running for your consideration. You can focus a little more sharply by eliminating the ones that don't have the image you're after; if your item is bone china, you wouldn't run in a publication heavy on mail order sports equipment. An electric crock pot would be of doubtful appeal in a magazine devoted to automotive products, and so on.

When you have boiled the selection down to about six possibilities, test *all* of them if your budget permits. If your funds will buy only two ads, *pick the pair of publications you think are best for your ad.* You can try others later.

Be sure to work out a code that enables you to determine where orders are coming from. This can be done by making small changes somewhere in your address from ad to ad. One might say, *Attn: Suite 4,* the other could read, *Attn: Room 4.* If the ad includes a coupon for buyers to cut out and mail, a tiny symbol imprinted somewhere within the coupon will tell you its origin.

If you plan to spend a substantial amount of money on your opening media campaign, you might entertain the idea of working with a small advertising agency. They make a fifteen percent commission on everything you spend for ad space. This commission is paid to them *by* the publications, so it costs you *nothing extra* to let them make the space buys for you. Plus, you can get professional advice on which magazines and newspapers might be most effective for you. Remember, an important part of an ad agency's business is knowing media. It can save you precious time and money to use one.

GETTING PROFESSIONAL LAYOUT, DESIGN, AND COPY SERVICES ABSOLUTELY FREE

The stakes in mail order are too big to allow compromise. But a quick look through any magazine that carries extensive mail order advertising will reveal ads—expensive ones—that were obviously prepared by amateurs. The copy is weak and clumsy, the illustrations, or photography is poorly executed, and the overall visual impact is ineffective.

When you go through the precaution of test marketing products and the expenses of sending out a mailing and purchasing costly media space, the ad you finally run must be completely professional. It must reach out of the page and grab the viewer by the eyes. Every word must be right, every last nuance must be planned to perfection. It takes a pro to do this.

If you engage the services of an advertising agency to make media recommendations and buys for you, it can create a hard-hitting, polished ad for you as part of its service. It will get maximum punch in the smallest possible ad . . . a necessity with today's soaring advertising costs.

If you do not use an agency, you would be wise to pay a qualified expert to develop your ad.

Whatever you do, don't let the ad become the weak link in your campaign! You are at the threshold of mail order success when you begin your media campaign. A strong ad is the last bridge to cross.

TAKING A CLOSER LOOK AT MAIL ORDER COSTS AND PROFITS

In most books that have been published on the subject of mail order, there are invariably pages and pages of formulas and theories that undoubtedly discourage more would-be business operators than they help. Here, we will keep it simple and brief.

When you determine your cost per sale from mailings and media advertising and when you know how much your average profit will be on each order, the business of planning future promotions becomes a matter of utmost simplicity.

In a mailing program, simply list every expense, just the way this example shows:

10,000 circulars, mailing envelopes, and reply envelopes	$250
Bulk rate postage	770
Preparation and handling	150
Approximate total expenses	$1,170

If you get a four percent return (using, of course, your own customer list) and each order you receive averages $12 gross—giving you a profit, conservatively speaking, of $7, this would be the result:

400 orders (4% return) at $7 profit per order	$2,800
Less expenses for mailing out orders (estimated 50¢ via parcel post)	200
Less original mailing expenses	1,170
Net profit	$1,430

While your actual expenses and/or profits could vary considerably from those shown above, the fact remains that you will not achieve wealth strictly on the strength of a direct mail program. However it can and will produce income for you, and it will further prove the value of your merchandise.

In this particular case, you know that you have a cost of $117 per thousand mailers, and that each thousand you mail will bring in approximately $480 in gross sales, and at least $280 in profits; an expenditure of $117 earns a net of $163. Not bad, but the jackpot lies in *media* advertising, as mentioned before. Here's an actual case:

Ads in four mail order publications	$2,295
Cost of ad preparation (major portion done by ad agency at no extra cost)	125
Approximate total expenses	$2,420

The combined circulation of these four monthly magazines was well over 35 million people. Here were the results:

```
1,788 orders at an average gross of $11.95
each (profit averaged $8.50 per order)  .......... $15,198
Less expenses for mailing out orders  .............  1,838
                                                    $13,360
Less original media and ad preparation cost  ......  2,420
    Net profit  ...............................     $10,940
```

A profit of nearly $11,000 for a new mail order venture gave this operator plenty of reason to rejoice. But more important, this first experience paved the way for bigger, easier profits to come.

In analyzing the figures, it turned out that three of the four magazines had done almost all the business. And of the three products advertised, one was of marginal popularity. So in the following campaign, ads were placed in the strongest *three* magazines, and only the *two* strongest items were offered, giving each larger space in the ads. The results looked like this:

```
Ads in three proven magazines  .................. $1,770
Cost of ad revisions  ..............................  95
    Total expenses  ...........................    $1,865
```

The repeated exposure brought virtually the same response as the first campaign in spite of the elimination of the weakest publication. The small increase was very likely due to the expanded emphasis on two products that were established bestsellers. This is what happened:

```
1,828 orders  ................................. $15,538
Less expenses for mailing out orders  .............. 914
                                                 $14,624
Less original media and ad cost  .................  1,865
    Net profit  ...............................   $12,759
```

This operator managed to dramatically increase profits by merely evaluating the effectiveness of his media and acting accordingly. And he now knows that if he spends about $620 for an ad in a *proven* publication and advertises *proven* merchandise, he can count heavily on bringing in a gross of over $7,000 and a profit of about $5,000. This ad would bring him 596 orders, and his cost per sale would be in the area of $1.05. Healthy, to say the least! He could continue to do this as long as he was able to continually locate, test, and prove new items.

Only four splashes a year would give this mail order operator an income EXCEEDING $50,000!

MAIL ORDER RULES THAT *MUST* BE FOLLOWED TO TAP IMMENSE PROFITS

Here are some of the most important guidelines to follow in building the mail order facet of your home merchandising business:

1. Mail customer orders *fast!* Even if you must hire temporary help, do everything you can to get orders in the mail *no later than twenty-four hours after you receive them!* One of the major complaints against many mail order firms is their apparent indifference to promptness in making deliveries.

   For orders under $20, top business people *do not* hold orders until personal checks clear. The excellent service this creates far outweighs the risk of occasional bad checks.

2. Every time you mail an order to a customer, it should include a *follow-up circular* that offers other items in your line. Such a flyer can be as simple and inexpensive as the original one. You're paying postage to send the order, so why not get a free ride on additional advertising? The extra business this brings might amaze you!

3. Honor merchandise returns quickly, without question. If a customer returns your items and requests a refund within a reasonable length of time (two or three weeks is fair), accept the return and promptly mail a full refund. The good will you build will more than compensate for the lost business (aside from good will, federal law makes such refunds mandatory!)

4. Take care of complaints as rapidly as you can. If merchandise is defective, replace it at no extra charge, and give your customer the benefit of the doubt if it appears that

the damage was done *after* delivery was made. This also should be within a reasonable length of time only.

5. Mailings and media advertising should be planned strategically to occur during the months that have traditionally yielded the best results. The sequence below is favorable to a number of successful operators (best month listed first, and so on down the line):

January	August	April
February	July	December
September	March	May
October	November	June

This is, of course, highly variable. It is meant only to provide a general guideline. Your actual experience may very well change the sequence.

6. When mailing or advertising to get seasonal business, *plan well ahead!* Most publications require four, five, and six weeks advance notice, and sometimes even more. September and October are effective for Christmas season buying, and these ads might have to be in the hands of the publication as early as July.

7. Always be aware of holidays and major events when planning your campaign. Do *not* attempt to compete with them! The world series, the superbowl game, Memorial Day, and similar events should be carefully avoided.

8. Mail to your entire list from no less than every four months to as often as once every two months. This establishes you firmly in the minds of your customers. Media ads should be run in *every issue,* if possible, until results begin to decline. When that happens, introduce new items and repeat the process.

9. Represent your product honestly. Be absolutely explicit about its size, color, and construction material. This will keep you clear of grief in the future.

HOW BERT M. STUMBLED INTO
AN OCEAN OF MONEY BY PURE CHANCE

Bert M. had been successfully running his own mobile showroom merchandising business for fourteen months when he bought the $4 ad that started him toward a mail order fortune.

This incredible story began when Bert placed a classified ad in a local newspaper for the purpose of selling off four picnic cooler chests that wouldn't fit into his small van. He admitted that buying them was a mistake because of their awkward size, and he was prepared to settle for a few dollars over his cost just to recover his investment.

On the day his ad ran, Bert was deluged with buyers. The chests had cost him $6 each, and he had advertised them at $8. They were gone in twenty minutes, but people rang his doorbell all day and well into that evening. They would have paid twice what he was asking if more chests had been available.

The surprised merchandiser didn't need much more encouragement than that to take this amazing development to its next logical step. He contacted the supplier and bought twenty-five more chests. Another classified ad went in for the following weekend offering the chests for $12.95. They sold out in five hours, a profit for Bert of $173.75 for practically no work at all.

Step three was a one-inch ad showing a picture of the chest, brief descriptive copy, and a selling price of $13.95. One hundred chests were stacked to the ceiling in his garage. Fifty-six of them were gone by Monday noon, and twenty-eight more were sold through the rest of the week—a net profit of around $650.

One-inch ads were then placed in every newspaper within a 200 mile radius. The chest was still offered at $13.95, but $1.50 was now required for postage and handling. Bert would no longer do business directly from his home - it was now strictly mail order. In a matter of five weeks, his gross sales were approaching *$2,000 every week!*

The new mail order specialist negotiated a $4.75 cost on large volume purchases of the chest, and he proceeded to place one-inch ads in thirty national publications. His personal income is nearly *$50,000 a year and climbing*. All this from four unwanted picnic coolers too big to peddle from his van!

PRICING AND PROFIT MARGINS
THAT HELP ASSURE MAIL ORDER SUCCESS

One of the challenges facing the mail order operator is the continuing necessity to acquire unique, appealing products that will bear profit margins of three to four times the cost price. The higher four times profit ratio is especially important when pricing items in the under $3 classification; the high overhead expenses in mail order demand that you price a $2 item in the $7 or $8 range rather than at 150%, which would be customary in most other aspects of merchandising.

Bigger ticket items can be successfully priced at three times cost, but seldom higher. For example, an item that costs you $6 can't be realistically priced at more than $17.95 without some danger of losing credibility in the eyes of the consumer. In Bert's case, a $4.75 item was marketed at $13.95, plus $1.50 for postage and handling, for a total ticket of $15.95. This was close enough to the three times profit mark to be comfortable, especially in view of the unusually low cost of his advertising program.

For your purposes as a merchandiser, mail order selling prices may be scattered in the $3.95 (around $1 cost) to $24.95 (around $8.50 cost) range, with items occasionally running as high as $29.95. This represents the most popular price range to the gift buying consumer.

The need for your products to be *unique* is stressed once again. When you price a given item at three to four times cost, you must be sure it isn't displayed on the shelves of every neighborhood store at much lower selling prices. Therefore, the product must be one that has not yet reached general popularity or one that has somehow escaped the attention of most merchants.

You now possess all the knowledge you need of the merchandising programs themselves. With these important guidelines, you know more than enough to start earning what may very well be the biggest money you've ever made before in your life. And as time goes on, you'll gain experience which will enchance your income even more.

But now we'll explore the area that *really* separates the pro's from the beginners: Just knowing how a certain sales program works does *not* guarantee success. It's the way you present merchandise to consumers that counts; it's your ability to pull customers in and your skill at compelling them to buy that truly makes the difference. That's called *merchandising*.

8

REMARKABLE MERCHANDISING STRATEGIES USED BY THE WORLD'S RICHEST OPERATORS

HOW EFFECTIVE MERCHANDISING
ROCKETED JOHN F's BUSINESS INTO FINANCIAL ORBIT

The difference between a satisfactory business operation and one which generates tremendous wealth is often the way merchandising is handled.

When John F. entered party plan and direct sales, he did it with adequate capital and a sound working knowledge in the art of selling. John started with a vast line of proven sellers and with more than enough skill to assure success. But his initial results were quite ordinary.

Like all too many business people, John was sure that it was enough merely to offer products to consumers. He never really gave a thought to *how* they should be offered. After two years of watching much smaller operations surpass his performance, the frustrated merchandiser started to do some serious thinking about his business.

The first thing this concerned businessman did was to visit several department stores. He was almost bowled over by the barrage of merchandising strategies that came at him from every direction.

These stores did *not* just set out their goods and wait for shoppers to get the buying whim; they used every conceivable gimmick to make the consumer buy. It was difficult to stroll down an aisle without being tempted to make a purchase. It was a lesson that changed the direction of his life.

John immediately incorporated the big store strategies into his party plan and direct sales operations. His gross volume more than doubled within 30 days, and his profits tripled! He discovered that the same merchandising tricks used by the retailing giants worked in his comparatively small enterprise.

The following pages give you the money-making tactics that John F. had to learn the hard way.

THE LOSS LEADER ATTRACTS BIG BUYING CUSTOMERS LIKE A POWERFUL MAGNET

One of the things that made a powerful impression on John F. during his memorable department store tour was their ability to draw him toward a display and bring him to the threshold of a purchase in an instant. This, he determined, was accomplished primarily through the use of loss leaders.

A loss leader is any product in your line which is temporarily priced below normal retail. This is done to attract customer attention. To make it as attractive as possible to consumers, the item is priced in the vicinity of your cost; therefore the word "loss" (you'll make little or no profit). "Leader" means both that it is designed to *lead* your product line in ads and displays and that buyers are *led* into your line through the appeal of the specialty priced item.

To measure up as a loss leader, a product must have these qualities:

1. It must be easily identifiable in terms of value. Customers must quickly see the savings to be gained by buying it. If an item of obscure worth is offered at a sizzling price, it won't do you much good as a loss leader since consumers probably have no idea what they're getting. But a popular item of known value which is priced well below going retails will do the trick.

2. It must be a "wanted" item of wide appeal. The most spectacular price won't be significant unless it's a product people are looking for.

3. Your loss leader must be in a price category that people can readily pay. An $89.95 oven broiler reduced to $40 is great, but how many shoppers would be tempted by that price? On the other hand, a $25 cassette tape recorder reduced to $15 would certainly stir people up.

The point in using loss leaders is this:

Under normal circumstances you can't expect customers to walk up to you and start buying. First they must be given a good reason for making a purchase — and a fabulous value or two (loss leaders) will provide that reason.

Now, you certainly don't want to be in business and spend your time selling products near your cost — even if it does double or triple the number of customers you attract. So let's take a look at how loss leaders can be turned into potent profit makers.

THE AMAZINGLY SIMPLE, INCREDIBLY EFFECTIVE STEP-UP

In retailing, a buyer who snatches up loss leaders is called a "cherry picker." As an astute merchandiser, your aim will be to make it virtually impossible for the cherry picker to do that. Clever shoppers of that description will see and be stimulated by your loss leader, then will encounter step-ups which will overwhelm the loss leader in appeal. Look at this example:

You decide to offer a line of alarm clocks. Your loss leader is a windup model that costs you $1.50 and retails at $3.49. To make it

Figure 10

hot, you offer it at your cost. But since you are not terribly anxious to sell anything at zero profit, you plan your line of clocks as shown in Figure 10.

Loss Leader

Your Cost $1.50
Suggested
Retail 3.98
Selling
Price 1.50

Step-Up "A"		Step-Up "B"	
Your Cost	$2.15	Your Cost	$3.00
Suggested Retail	4.98	Suggested Retail	6.98
Selling Price	2.75	Selling Price	4.95

Step-up "A" is intended to swing interest away from the $1.50 loss leader and get you a little profit. It's electric, has a lighted dial, and is more highly styled. For all these extra features, the customer pays just a little more than you are asking for the loss leader.

Step-up "B" has everything "A" has, plus a snooze alarm, lots of gadgets and very smart design. It's extremely tempting when compared to the loss leader — and your margin is almost respectable.

While loss leaders *demand* the use of step-ups, *every* product category you carry should be planned to make the shopper buy better, higher priced merchandise. In other words, by spending just a little more money, the buyer can get an item that looks far better than the one you feature. And in the process, you make bigger profits.

These are the basic rules to use in handling your step-ups:

1. *Don't* display them as prominently as you do the loss leader. They should be shown to each customer, but only after that shopper asks about the loss leader. When presented in such a low-pressure manner, the step-up will often sell itself.

2. The step-up should be only a little more money than the item you are stepping from — but should look and perform measurably better. You must make the jump in price as easy to take for your customer as you can.

3. The step-up must, of course, be in the same product category as the loss leader. A customer will be strongly inclined to jump from one clock to another, more deluxe model. But will usually not jump from the basic clock to a fishing reel.

BEWARE OF THE "NAIL DOWN"

If you use the magnetic power of the loss leader and the step-up, you must be prepared to sell a number of products at abnormally low profit margins. The cherry pickers will prevail sometimes no matter how adept your merchandising happens to be. This is simply the price you pay for increased customer activity.

Therefore, you are urged to carry a sufficient stock of loss leaders to satisfy customer demand. One of the incidents most irritating to buyers is when they are unable to buy the featured item.

Some unscrupulous dealers use "nail downs." These are loss leaders which are *never* sold to customers under any circumstances. A department store chain offered a washer and dryer at a price far below competition. When customers responded, they were immediately led to more costly step-ups. The advertised set was downgraded by the store's salespeople, and the machines sampled in the store were scratched and dirty.

If there's a sure way to damage the reputation of a business, it's through unsavory tactics like these. If you offer products at low prices, by all means be ready to deliver exactly what you promise, profitable or not. Use the step-up to improve profits, *not* for devious merchandising practices!

THE ONE DOLLAR OFFER ATTRACTS HUGE SPENDING WHERE OTHER STRATEGIES FAIL

If you offer a six piece manicure set for $1 with the purchase of a $14.95 facial sauna, its a bargain hard for shoppers to resist. A foam rubber pillow for $1 with the purchase of a $12.95 blanket is also tough to pass.

In the first example, you'd have around $6.50 in cost for the sauna and $2 at the most for the manicure set. A profit of $7.45 despite the fact that it sounds like a give-away. The pillow might run you $3, the blanket $6, for a total of $9 in cost. You sell the set for $13.95 ($12.95 plus the dollar) giving you a net profit of $4.95. Not bad considering the appeal of the offer.

This is one more form of leader, but one that consistently generates decent profits. If you wish, it can be structured more spectacularly than in the above example: The secondary item might be offered for *one cent* instead of one dollar, or the primary item can be discounted even more deeply.

If you decide to use this strong merchandising strategy, keep this in mind: The secondary product (the one offered for the smaller amount) is usually the element that commands the consumer's attention. Therefore, it might be of little or no advantage to price the primary item below its usual retail price. People will be riveted to that one dollar price, and will scarcely notice the bigger price on the larger item.

Another point to remember is that one cent tends to cheapen a product, where one dollar lets it retain a semblance of value. So be careful when setting up the promotion. Testing it both ways might be advisable to see how your customers react.

This method is extremely effective when both the primary and secondary items are related as are the manicure set and the facial sauna (both beauty care products), and the blanket/pillow combination. But it can work as well if the two products are totally unrelated. You might, for example, offer the one dollar item with *any* purchase from your line that meets or exceeds a pre-established retail amount. Whether the price you establish is $19.95, $29.95 or $49.95, be sure it's enough to protect your profit. But it must, at the same time, be appealing and competitive.

You can run several one-dollar offers simultaneously and change them periodically to keep them interesting for shoppers. Or you can use this promotion as an occasional special or whatever you see fit to do. In any event, you will find that it stirs up customer interest and boosts your dollar volume.

HOW CORA E. USES ACTION TO SUCCESSFULLY MARKET $38,000 A YEAR IN COSTUME JEWELRY

Two years after she was widowed, Cora E. started a party plan business, then branched out into direct sales. She carried a variety of popular general merchandise ranging from housewares to personal items including fragrances and leather goods. The merchandising tactic that tripled her business came suddenly and unexpectedly.

For two dollars Cora bought a castoff three-tiered lazy susan that slowly revolved when plugged into a socket. She thought the old jewelry store display would be effective for displaying small pieces. At that price, it was certainly worth a try!

Cora sanded down the piece and spray painted it. Then, at her next showing, she loaded its shelves with items. When the time came to display, she plugged it in and started it turning. The products displayed this new way outsold all others by a noticeable margin. It might have been a coincidence, but Cora was sure that the motion made the difference.

From that almost accidental beginning as a clever merchandiser, Cora went deeply into the use of action to help sell products. She used balloons, streamers, mirrors, and any other gimmick she could think of that would animate and bring her display to life. The first try was no fluke after all; motion and color did tremendously increase the woman's volume.

In the direct sales aspect of her operation, action was a somewhat more challenging objective. Cora finally came up with two ideas that did the trick: First, she had a lazy susan specially made that was much more compact than her first one and designed to be carried easily. It's perfect for quickly displaying small items in a home. The other idea is a battery operated high-intensity lamp that dramatically highlights any product she wants to feature. It brings depth and sparkle to items — especially jewelry.

Cora now has an almost theatrical flair for action merchandising . . . and it pays off in bigger cash profits.

THE PRIVATE SALE:
ANOTHER STEPPING STONE TO PROSPERITY

A small retail clothing store closes its doors to normal walk-in trade for three days on two occasions every year. During those periods, the owner closes his shop all day, then opens from 6:00 p.m. to midnight . . . but only to old customers and guests who have been *invited*. During each six-hour period, *ushers have to control the crowd waiting in line to enter the store!*

You don't have to be a storekeeper to make the private sale produce miraculous income. You can operate as effectively as the retailer can by simply renting a room, inviting your total list of customers — plus choice prospects, and holding a private sale of your own over a two, three, or four day period.

The basic ingredients for success are these:

1. You must have a substantial customer list in order to make the private sale work. Several merchandisers report getting a 10% response to invitations. Therefore, if you mail to 3,000 people, you can expect as many as 300 eager buyers.

2. The people you invite must be within reasonable distance of your sale location. Don't expect them to travel more than one hour to attend.

3. In your invitation, you must be absolutely clear about date, time, and location of the sale (include a map if possible). It's also important to list several spectacular sample buys; your customers must get a taste of the bargains available. To accomplish this, you can establish a number of loss leaders and step-ups as described earlier.

4. Here are several other tricks that attract big crowds to private sales:

   a. Emphasize in big, bold letters that the event is for customers *only,* and the general public is *not* invited.

   b. Limit purchases: Say, "ONE TO A CUSTOMER" in your copy on a sprinkling of items. This, of course, conveys a feeling of limited stock which creates a sense of buying urgency.

   c. In the invitation, instruct the customer that admission to the sale will be granted only if the invitation is presented at the door. This makes the guest feel as if the event is exclusive.

5. Finally, don't overdo the private sale idea. If repeated too frequently, it will almost certainly lose its value and appeal. Twice yearly seems ideal to many home business operators.

The hours you select do not necessarily have to be the same as the clothing store's 6:00 p.m. to midnight time. Plan it for any hours you feel will work best for your particular clientele; it is important to be open for business when people are not working.

THE TREMENDOUS POWER OF THE FREE GIFT: DAVID C's FORTUNE FORMULA

Although he isn't in a home merchandising business, David C. nevertheless has proven beyond any shadow of a doubt the power of gifts - and has demonstrated his extraordinary ability as a business builder. He conducts a temporary help agency which is only in its second year of operation. Despite the newness of the business, it has already outdistanced much older firms in terms of volume and profits.

David's breathtaking success is mainly attributable to one factor: He sends out mailers on a monthly basis - and every single one includes either a free gift or a coupon which can be used to obtain one. Here are just a few of the gift ideas he has used:

1. A coffee mug with his company name imprinted on it.
2. A novelty pencil with erasers on both ends. Again, imprinted.
3. A small pencil with an eraser that must be at least five inches long.
4. A miniature cultivator for house plants.

The list goes on and on. Dave rarely passes up a free gift idea. His customers have come to expect these items from him, and they love them. The lowest price he'll spend is around 20¢ per item, the maximum is in the neighborhood of 70¢ (the coffee mug). Regardless of price, almost every give-away David uses gets tremendous response and a slew of new customers.

So if you think low-priced novelties are disdained by consumers, think again. The giving of free gifts is one of the most powerful merchandising devices known. The value of the gift is *not* of significance; it's the *uniqueness* that makes the impression.

No matter which home merchandising business you have decided to operate, free gifts will fit. Here are just a few of the ways they can be used:

1. You can give a gift in the lower price range (20¢ to 35¢) to *every* prospective customer whether he makes a purchase or not.
2. You can give a better gift (35¢ to 70¢) to every buying customer only. This can either be instead of the above gift or in addition to it.

The possibilities of giving free gifts are limited only by your imagination. This merchandising strategy comes as close to being indispensible as any described in this book.

MODELING: THE WAY JUDY M. GETS SALES
IN THE BLINK OF AN EYE

Movement and color are vital dimensions in the art of merchandising. Bringing items to life will sell them faster than any other means at your disposal. Judy M., an especially adept party plan operator, discovered that modeling is the most direct way to give products dramatic impact.

After six months in her party plan business, Judy was reasonably satisfied with sales and profits. She specialized in jewelry and personal decor items like leather goods, fragrances, and various other appearance accessories. The young business was already providing her well over $300 a week in net income and showed signs of gradual growth.

One evening during a home showing, one the guests asked Judy if she could try on a pair of jade earrings. The request itself wasn't unusual, but Judy had never heard the reason before. The woman told Judy that certain gemstones tended to change colors against her skin, and she wanted to be sure the earrings complemented her coloring. She tried them on, and Judy proceeded to sell six sets of earrings from her jade collection!

By focusing the attention of the entire group on the modeling activity, sales multiplied. Watches, pendants, bracelets, rings, purses, and other personal decor items were displayed by guests and thus "came to life" before the other buyers.

Colognes and perfumes were demonstrated in the same way. The guests could see how various fragrances reacted to different skin chemistries. In this area, too, sales climbed rapidly.

Judy immediately made modeling — or guest participation as she prefers to call it — a basic part of every showing. Each item in her line is tried on and shown to the group as it would be worn in actual use. Sales have nearly doubled since this simple merchandising strategy was first employed.

The biggest problem encountered by this skillful party plan operator is reluctance on the part of guests to model in front of others. But this is easily overcome with the help of a little gentle, good natured prodding by Judy. If necessary, she offers a free gift to all volunteers, and that usually breaks down the initial shyness.

Regardless of the type of merchandise you carry, don't miss the opportunity to bring customers into the demonstration process. Even if you're in direct sales — and there are no other people present except you and the prospect — urge the potential buyer to try on or at least touch and handle the products you are carrying.

HOW THE "BARGAIN DUMP" CAN PRODUCE RICHES FOR YOU

Here's an ingenious merchandising trick that was pioneered and perfected by food supermarkets. It's remarkable because *it is pure illusion!* There is *no* special pricing required, and *no* effort at all needed on your part. Yet, it is one of the most powerful merchandising tactics ever devised.

The next time you do your food shopping, notice that scattered throughout the market are a number of big baskets or giant cardboard boxes filled with products. These large bins are usually brimming with items that appear to be haphazardly emptied into the container. Attached to the bins are signs which announce "NOW ONLY $2.98 EACH," or "98¢ WHILE THEY LAST," or something similar.

The effect on the shopper, of course, is that the huge container, or "dump," holds items that have been ruthlessly discounted by the store. The fact is, the same products could be, and usually are, displayed just an aisle or two away *at the same regular prices shown on the bin!* But the customer wants to believe that anything so carelessly displayed by the store *must* be priced much, much lower than it usually sells for. And it never occurs to most people to check the dump item prices against the identical stock neatly arranged on a nearby shelf!

So buyers tend to grab items out of the dumps compulsively. They have absolute faith that they are getting the bargain of a lifetime even though the sign simply states a price, without mention of a special or discount.

It is a fact that bargain dumps outsell products displayed in conventional ways. And it is a fact that you, the home merchandiser, can use it to cash in the same way supermarkets do:

1. At home merchandise showings, you can use an ordinary carton to hold dozens of items. It should look as if the box was just opened and recently arrived from the factory.

    If the box is too large for the number of products you want to use in it, a false bottom can easily be made to reduce the volume of the box.

2. The mobile showroom merchandiser can very effectively use dumps in conjunction with regular product displays. Remember to make the sign big enough to be seen by passing motorists and pedestrians.

Certain merchandisers feel that the dump technique is most effective when one box holds many of just one kind of item (Figure 11). Others use a wide variety of products in the same dump and encourage customers to browse through the contents. You should test both ways to see which works best for you.

Figure 11

PUT THE MIRACULOUS IMPACT OF IMPULSE-APPEAL TO WORK FOR YOU
THE WAY IT DOES FOR MAJOR SUPERMARKETS

The bargain dump is successful because it has enormous impulse-appeal; it practically reaches out for the customer and says, "buy me . . . I'm irresistible!" Impulse purchases make up a significant part of a store's total volume — and a substantial portion of its profits. It's an area that is extremely important to the overall merchandising effort.

Impulse-appeal is not intangible. It's not a magical quality that occurs unpredictably. It can be planned and measured to get precisely the results you want. When a store manager stacks pre-packaged donuts at each check-out counter, he or she knows within close limits how many hundreds of packages will be grabbed by customers in the line. And after a short time, *you* will know how many dollars will be generated by your impulse-appeal strategies.

To make impulse-appeal work as effectively as it should, several basic rules must be followed. Here they are:

1. The item must be priced in the pocket change category. In other words, its total cost should be a sum that most people would consider incidental. This, in most instances, would encompass any price up to around $3. If priced much beyond that point, the buyer's impulse to make a purchase is disrupted by a decision-making process which will work against you. Your objective is to make the purchase happen without forcing the customer to think.

2. The product should be carefully selected by you. Every impulse-appeal item must be just different enough to seize the eye of the shopper. A keychain attached to a compass; a pocket tool kit; a miniature stapler; an electronic calcaulator stand all are items that people would not usually buy during routine shopping. There are literally thousands of products just unique enough to qualify for the impulse-appeal category.

3. All impulse-appeal displays are set up in locations that command the attention of the shopper. In party plan and mobile showroom merchandising, your impulse-appeal items are scattered among the products in your regular line. In direct sales, you carry small boxes which are reserved for impulse items. In direct mail, they are dispersed among higher priced merchandise throughout your mailer or catalog.

4. Impulse displays must be designed to draw the attention of the prospect. In addition to the dump display, these items may be hung on cards, placed atop platforms, or featured in any other way that catches the shopper's eye.

When these rules are followed, your impulse selections will provide astonishing profits; they will consistently lead or be very close to your highest priced items in profitability, even though many more of them have to be sold to match the dollar volume of those bigger purchases.

MARK G's ASTRONOMICAL PROFITS THROUGH SPECIAL PROMOTIONS

The power of anticipating and taking advantage of various holidays and buying seasons cannot be overemphasized. Mark G., an insurance agent, does little more than that to make an extra $27,000 a year as a part-time merchandiser.

Mark's whopping side income is made by working several weeks of each year. But the weeks he puts in are the ones when most of the year's buying is done by consumers.

- *During the Christmas Season* he begins around October 10 and operates a mail order and direct sales operation until around December 20.
- *Before Easter* he conducts business for approximately three weeks.
- *For Mother's Day and Father's Day* he carries appropriate products to serve gift needs.
- *For Memorial Day and the Fourth of July* he takes full advantage of summer vacation demand by selling huge quantities of sunglasses, camping equipment, sporting goods, and other related products.
- *For High School and College Graduation Time* he specializes in watches and other gifts which are popular for those age categories.

Every successful merchandiser is extremely alert with respect to the calendar. Buying and other preparation must be done far enough in advance to assure readiness when prime selling time arrives. Those special dates which roll around every year have a way of coming up rapidly. If you're ready, you'll make the most of them as Mark does!

WAYS TO GET A FORTUNE IN FREE ADVERTISING

Whatever you do, *don't* overlook free publicity for your business! Hundreds of extra buyers would gladly patronize you if they knew you existed. One very good way to let them know about your business is via local publications of various types.

Neighborhood newspapers, for example, almost always want to print items about interesting developments in the community.

Many of them would consider the starting of a new business worthy of free space. Such publicity can do nothing but help you. But when you add a pinch of merchandising flair to this simple announcement, you have yourself a hard-hitting message that will bring in big business. This is how it's done:

One way to get the attention of newspapers in no uncertain terms is to come up with a totally unique product that would be of genuine interest to people. Don't worry if it has limited appeal; its real value will be in its newsworthiness. This, combined with an announcement of your new enterprise, gives a local newspaper strong justification for printing an article about you. In such cases, you might well have the opportunity of providing a photograph of the unusual product . . . and of yourself also.

One other excellent possibility for free publicity lies in the area of churches, organizations, and clubs. They are extremely active in fund raising activities. These functions almost always require gift donations. When you make such donations, you can usually get your money's worth of publicity in newsletters, bulletins, or other types of house organs.

One more good idea is a gift give-away program through the same organizations mentioned above. Many groups like this try to assist families during the Christmas season. They collect and distribute toys to poor children and generally attempt to bring needy people a little happiness. If you are in a position to award a group of products to an organization in your area, it will serve the dual purposes of helping people and bringing you community recognition.

Sound merchandising strategies *will* sell just about any product you want to sell, anywhere you want to sell it. But there are certain product categories that always seem to be extremely popular, and a few you would do well to avoid. The next chapter brings you priceless information about this.

9

PRODUCT CATEGORIES THAT ASSURE YOU OF HIGHLY PROFITABLE OPERATIONS

HOW NANCY A. GETS FREE EXPERT EVALUATIONS THAT GUARANTEE SOUND BUYING DECISIONS

In two years of buying and selling merchandise as a direct sales operator, Nancy A. can recall only three items that could definitely be classified as mistakes. Not bad at all, considering she has purchased well over 400 different products!

Her secret is this: Nancy will never make a commitment to purchase merchandise from a supplier until she has asked at least five consumers, and preferably as many as ten, their opinions about the item. She has learned that her own judgment can easily be distorted by personal prejudices in the process of buying; her own taste can get in the way of objective decisions.

Nancy simply obtains one sample of a product she is considering, and carries it with her on calls for several days. Each time she encounters a prospect who seems to have good instincts about merchandise, she produces the sample and asks if the person would be interested in it. She has developed the following check list in order to assure thorough product evaluations:

1. Nancy explains that the product is not for sale. This eliminates consumer resistance which could color a frank response; if the person knows the item can't be bought, he is much more apt to give an honest opinion.

2. Whether the individual likes the item or not, Nancy asks how much he thinks it should sell for. Knowing what her cost would be if she finally decided to add it to her line, Nancy gets a pretty good idea about its value at retail (more than a few items met with unanimous approval, but fell down badly due to unfavorable customer opinion about prices).

3. Each customer is queried as to why he likes or dislikes the item. On one occasion, Nancy was showing a sewing kit in red vinyl which received enthusiastic reaction. But the actual stock she would have to buy would be black vinyl, and customers were specific about their preference for red. She declined the item and probably averted an error.

There is no more qualified buying expert than the ultimate consumer. Only heaven knows how many businesses fail to achieve prosperity because the buyer remains the sole judge of merchandise and the customer's preferences are never taken into account.

9 GUIDELINES THAT BRING YOU WINNING SELECTIONS EACH AND EVERY TIME

In addition to the highly recommended strategy of getting consumer opinion on possible purchases, these steps will bring you even closer to establishing a perfect buying record:

1. *Is the product likely to be used by most people?* If it has limited appeal, be ready for limited sales and profits. But

if the item seems to have a place in the lives of the majority of customers you encounter, consider buying it.

2. *If it's a luxury, is it affordable?*
People will indulge themselves occasionally by spending more than they should on things they don't really need. But these moments of abandon do not occur often enough to make your business successful. Therefore, you must make sure that non-necessity items are priced within easy reach of your average customer. An automobile steering wheel cover, for example, might very well be popular at up to $3.98 retail, but would not have wide acceptance at $9.95.

3. *How does the product compare with those being sold currently by other outlets?*
If the product you are considering is already being merchandised in a similar shape, style, and price range, you would do well to carefully observe the current one to see how it's doing on the market. If it's selling, you must then be sure that the one you choose is competitive in price and quality.

4. *Is the product compatible with the balance of your merchandise line?*
As your business matures, your line will stabilize. It will settle into the product categories your customers show the greatest interest in. You might find yourself specializing in cookware or ceramics or toys or any of numerous other lines. At this time, you will want to be very careful about making purchases that are in wild contrast to your established categories (but not so careful that you fail to add an occasional exciting change of pace!)

5. *Will the product be continually available?*
Your position will be stronger in the long run if you can offer your customers continuity; they like to see items displayed one day and be able to buy them a month or two later. This gives you an image of solidity. While no supplier can guarantee that a particular product will still be produced months down the road, you nevertheless should get reasonable assurance it will be around for at least a little while.

Future availability is, indeed, important. But it isn't necessary in your total line. If you come across an exceptional product at an extraordinary price, by all means buy it, even if it's a one-time opportunity with no re-order possibilities.

6. *Is it safe?*
Take every precaution you can to assure that products are harmless. This is doubly true when it comes to toys and fragrances. A doll with eyes inserted by sharp, easily removed pins is an obvious hazard and should be avoided at any price. A cosmetic item with caustic tendencies is far too dangerous to consider.

7. *Is it of acceptable quality?*
The fact that you may not strive to deal in the finest merchandise available is no reason why you should not insist on solid workmanship. The world is virtually flooded with junk, and that is enough reason for you to shop until you see quality which measures up to the price you must pay.

8. *Will the future price be stable?*
Getting the supplier's word on future prices can be tricky in this age of volatile market forces. But try your best anyway. At least make an attempt to get a commitment from the vendor that re-orders won't be double the price of your initial order.

9. *Would the product be easy to dump?*
If, after all the precautions you take, the item still turns out to be a slow seller, you want to have the ability to recover at least your initial cost. You can dump a buying error easily enough if you price it low—and if it has at least some attractiveness. But if it's atrocious beyond description, you might not even be able to give it away.

SPECIALTY MERCHANDISE: A LADDER TO FABULOUS EARNINGS

Americans spend billions of dollars every year on a product category called specialty merchandise. It is characterized by colorful, low-priced novelty items that have strong impulse appeal.

Here are a few of the product types that come under the specialty merchandise heading:

Keychains
Change purses

Watchbands
Plastic toys
Gag gifts
Jewelry (inexpensive costume variety)
Flashlights
Combs, and comb and brush sets
Low-priced home decor items
Automotive accessories and novelties
Small tool sets
Sunglasses

There are probably a few hundred others. As you can see, specialty merchandise covers a vast amount of territory. It's offered in stores of virtually every type and by countless individuals engaged in various merchandising activities. It is purchased by consumers in every corner of America and throughout the world.

Specialty merchandise is generally packaged for maximum impulse punch. It sometimes comes in transparent polybags stapled to printed cardboard "headers" which have round holes for hanging on display rack pegs. You see these displays almost every time you go shopping (Figure 12.)

Figure 12

The polybag and header is a typical specialty merchandise packaging technique.

Another popular packaging method for this category is the conventional paper box, color printed to attract shopper attention. In some cases, the box has a transparent window which permits examination of the product. If the item in question is rather small, such as a keychain, it can be carded. In this packaging method, a display card usually holds one dozen identical items, and the consumer simply takes one off to make a purchase. The card can be hung, or set up on an easel for counter display (Figure 13).

Figure 13

Carded specialty merchandise saves you the expense of packaging each item and has strong visual impact on the shopper.

Bulk packaging is gaining in popularity with specialty merchandise operators. Here, a particular item is packed in quantity in a simple carton. This permits the lowest possible prices because there are no printing costs or other packaging materials to consider. Merchandise available in bulk can either be offered by you in dump displays (see preceding chapter) or re-packaged in polybags or boxes which are easily and inexpensively obtained through commercial paper companies.

As a general rule, specialty merchandise fits in the under $5 price category, and most of it is under $2 at retail. It is safe to say that virtually every item in this classification can be described as having exceptional impulse-appeal (or should).

You can't go very far wrong by concentrating your efforts on specialty merchandise. It has enjoyed unprecedented popularity for decades and shows absolutely no signs of losing its position of preeminence. Two basic cautions are: 1) Be sure you're buying it at the lowest possible prices, and 2) try to avoid duplicating the products carried by local stores and competitive dealers.

RICK J's MOBILE CLOTHING BUSINESS:
HIS OPPORTUNITIES AND PROBLEMS

His "store" is a van modified to hold two rods which run the length of the interior. On these, Rick can hang a tremendous stock of pants, shirts, jackets, and dresses. He claims that his inventory is almost as large and diverse as that found in a small neighborhood shop.

In the manner of the traditional mobile showroom merchandiser, Rick selects a location near an industrial concentration or in an area heavily traveled by automobile or pedestrian traffic. He displays a few of his outstanding styles outside the truck along with several signs announcing specials and does business that nets him $27,000 a year (he'll soon begin direct merchandising of his clothing line which should, by his estimate, provide an additional $10,000 at least).

But this hefty income is not without its headaches; Rick spends several hours each week adjusting customer complaints. These problems range from loose buttons to sloppy sewing by the factory. Quite often he finds it necessary to take garments back to his suppliers on a customer's behalf. If difficulties cannot be resolved, Rick will fully refund the money and absorb the loss.

This merchandiser works as hard, or harder, than a regular retail dealer in maintaining perfect customer relations. He claims that this effort costs him at least eight percent of his total dollar volume. At times he has been tempted to drop clothing in favor of some kind of less troublesome merchandise category, but he hasn't found a satisfactory alternative. Rick is philosophical about the rather tricky business of keeping consumers satisfied; he feels that a good income and personal freedom are worth extra effort.

Clothing can, indeed, be extremely lucrative. But Rick says there are certain essential rules that must be followed to make it pay:

1. You must learn as much as possible about the construction and styling of clothing *before* you attempt to sell it. Customers will ask questions, and you have to be able to answer them!

2. The style preferences of your customers must be understood. Rick explained that one of the secrets to his success is in refusing to purchase certain styles just because he has received a few isolated requests for them. The clothing merchandiser will wisely base his or her line on the majority preference. Rick quickly learned that he could not please everyone.

3. The customer must be assured that you will be available to stand in back of the purchase. And buyers must have every confidence that you will take care of problems, no matter how small they may seem.

4. Accessories such as ties, socks and undergarments are important extra profit-makers for clothing merchandisers. Rick says it's important to show the accessories to each and every shopper.

If you are willing to provide first-class service and a full measure of followup on all your sales, clothing might be an excellent merchandise choice for you.

FRAGRANCES AND COSMETICS: THE SURFACE OF THIS MULTI-BILLION DOLLAR CATEGORY HASN'T BEEN SCRATCHED

Men are buying aftershave lotions, colognes, talcs, and other toiletries at a record rate. Women are buying perfumes, colognes and a seemingly endless array of beauty products at a dramatically increasing pace. The profits in this field are nearly unbelievable, but it's just the beginning.

The special strength of cosmetics is that they fit well with practically any other category you carry. They are compatible with clothing, specialty merchandise, home decor, and most others. Or, they constitute a powerful line by themselves. They are equally appealing to men and women alike, and they are just about free of the service considerations present with other products. Finally, they are consumed, and therefore replaced by the customer at some point after the purchase.

Cosmetics are most effectively marketed through party plan, direct sales, or mobile showroom merchandising. In other words, through the methods that put you face to face with the consumer. Mail order would be minimally effective because the shopper can't sample the product.

The merchandising possibilities in fragrances are enormous: Many lines can be purchased from suppliers who will provide your own private label on bottles (an example earlier in this book described how this is accomplished). Private labels give your business exclusivity and also minimize comparison shopping by consumers.

But the most powerful merchandising tactic that applies to selling cosmetics and fragrances is the personal demonstration; every potential buyer can sample various products. And beauty aids such as lipsticks, eye shadow, and nail polishes can also be tried before they are purchased. This never fails to be entertaining, and it almost always sells lots of items.

Profit margins of four to five times cost are not at all unusual in cosmetics. Therefore, you can offer good quality at prices that are competitive with widely advertised brands. One more favorable point is the compactness of this category. Many samples can be carried in a comparatively small amount of space.

Experts say that one of the main areas of concern in cosmetics sales is the sensitivity of skin; certain customers might be allergic to various components in perfumes or other products. This can lead to problems unless you take the trouble to question your prospects before letting them sample or buy your items. Ask them if they have ever had adverse reactions before. If so, you should recommend that they consult a physician before taking a chance. Many lines include non-allergenic fragrances which are specially compounded to be harmless for people with such sensitivity.

One very enterprising perfume manufacturer has developed a spectrum of fragrances, each one closely emulating a renown internationally known brand. These thinly disguised imitations sell for a fraction of what the originals cost, and the public has eagerly accepted them. This illustrates the profit power of this dynamic merchandise area and the ease of making sales.

THE BOOMING FIELD OF JEWELRY AND PERSONAL ACCESSORIES

Better quality jewelry runs a close second to specialty merchandise in popularity—and is almost equal to cosmetics in profitability—among direct-to-consumer operators. Inexpensive jewelry actually comes under the specialty merchandise classification, but higher grade merchandise should be considered a category of its own.

"Better quality" should be defined: Rings from around $25 to $70 retail; watches from $20 to $75 retail and pendants from $15 to $50 retail would generally typify the moderately priced jewelry group. These pieces usually have genuine semi precious stones— or good imitations, with gold-filled settings.

This particular range is exceptionally popular because the craftsmanship is clearly superior to low-priced pieces, and the styling is strongly influenced by expensive jewelry. Therefore, you have the best of both worlds, and you can be proud to show these products to your customers.

Non-jewelry personal accessories will blend very well with your jewelry line and will sell as vigorously. This includes purses, wallets, and other quality leather goods and could encompass jewelry boxes and small overnight luggage pieces. Here again, the lower price ranges in personal accessory items would come under the specialty merchandise category and would be made of imitation leather materials.

It would be advantageous for you to make an early decision about which way to go, specialty merchandise prices, or *better* jewelry and accessory prices. The two really do not mix well. A customer who is exposed to inexpensive jewelry pieces will not be easy to switch to better merchandise. An example of this is expecting a buyer to go from a $3.95 ring to one that is vastly superior at $24.95. You would do better, from a merchandising standpoint, to have the middle price range displayed, combined with a few fine pieces as step-ups. In other words, a switch from a ring at $24.95 to an outstanding one at $69.95.

Another factor that should go into your decision process is quality and service: Good middle price range jewelry should be made to last, thus providing your customer with real value. Specialty merchandise category jewelry all too often falls apart as the customer examines it!

So whether you decide to go low, middle, or high in jewelry and accessories, you'll find it an extremely profitable, very desirable area to be in. Interest is at a peak and promises to keep gaining.

NOSTALGIA PRODUCTS REAP RICHES FOR LOIS K.

Interest in yesterday has been growing in recent years. As life becomes more complicated, we crave symbols of a life that seemed much simpler.

Old comic books bring incredible prices at auctions; toys that go back decades are sometimes sold for thousands of dollars; even the clothing of past eras can bring windfalls. A number of merchandisers who watched this trend develop are now capitalizing on it. One of them is Lois K.

She is not an antique dealer, or a collector of momentos salvaged from dusty attics. Lois is a modern merchandiser who searches for *new* items which are re-creations of products popular during the 1920s and 30s. Her inventory is utterly fascinating, and at any given moment might consist of several of these categories:

Art deco era mirrored pictures

Simulated "Regulator" clocks

Tiffany-style table and hanging lamps

Reproductions of very old full-color posters

Accent chairs copied from turn-of-the-century designs

Throw pillows with a Victorian flavor

Bead strings for room dividers

Small stained glass panels (a few actually glass, but most of them plastic imitations)

Lois simply will not purchase items that are not related to the past. Her customers have come to expect this merchandise from her, and rarely buy nostalgia items elsewhere. The number of people who seek this taste of the past is growing rapidly, and Lois does not foresee any decline in demand.

The buying task is somewhat more complex for Lois than it is for most other merchandisers. She must locate these pieces one by one since there are very few suppliers who specialize in producing nostalgia goods. Therefore, she spends nearly two full days of every week making the rounds of importers, wholesalers, and jobber showrooms. She considers a buying trip successful if she locates one good reproduction at the right price and available in sufficient quantities.

This rather unusual selection of merchandise has proved to be extremely fruitful for Lois K. Her income at the end of one year in business was $19,200, and she has cleared almost that much already in the first seven months of her second year.

HOW PLANTS PRODUCE A BIG INCOME FOR LYNN J.

It started when a spider plant which was hanging over her patio crashed to the ground one windy day. Lynn thought nothing of it and swept up the pot fragments and dirt. Several weeks later, she saw the first traces of new spider plants growing from the ground nearby.

Within several months, they were growing out of control. So Lynn began potting and selling them at a local flea market on weekends. She gradually obtained different plant varieties, and her following continued to increase in size.

The landmark event in her remarkable career came when Lynn agreed to hold a plant show at a customer's house for the benefit of the woman's neighbors. 18 guests attended, and the new plant retailer sold out and went home with $187 in cash (her cost ran somewhere around $20!)

From that moment, Lynn's business has converted exclusively to party plan sales of plants. She works harder than most operators; the young lady puts in five evenings a week, plus Saturday or Sunday afternoon every week. She actually must refuse bookings because of the demand for her services. Lynn earns well over $40,000 a year.

The major problem Lynn faces in the marketing of plants is, of course, the occasional unpredictability of growing things. Plants are delicate and can be sensitive to frequent moving and handling. It has also become a highly competitive business; most food markets now carry a wide selection of house plants.

But even with the difficulties she must overcome, Lynn wouldn't consider being in any other line. She says that her key to success has been the giving of frank advice to customers. She guides people on the best types of plants for various light and temperature conditions, and she will not carry varieties that are difficult to grow. Lynn will also replace free of charge any plant that dies within 30 days of purchase. This liberal policy has contributed enormously to the profitability of her enterprise.

GIFTS AND HOME ACCESSORIES DO BILLIONS OF DOLLARS IN ANNUAL VOLUME. IT'S EASY TO GET YOUR FAIR SHARE

There was a time not that long ago when virtually all of the business done in gifts and home accessories went to department stores, with a handful of home business operators getting the overflow. In large part, this was due to the fact that there were fewer importers bringing goods in from world markets, and competition for top products was fierce.

Today, however, there are a far greater number of foreign and domestic factories producing gift type merchandise. And since importing is no longer the exclusive domain of large scale business operators, you now have almost every advantage that the major retailing chains had all to themselves just yesterday.

Along with jewelry, there is no more easy-to-sell category than home accessories (with the exception of specialty merchandise). It's a vast product area which allows the merchandiser to be as unique as an exclusive boutique shop. Your customers would select from items in your line that could not be duplicated in local stores—or in the displays of competing dealers. But uniqueness of this kind requires your constant alertness; you must get to know all importers in your area and be aware of what is being shown by the competition.

The gift and home accessory category includes any product that is used to adorn the interior of a residence or office (plants, by that definition, could also be considered home accessories). Here are just a few examples:

- *Glassware* could range from sets of drinking glasses to fine, hand-blown candy dishes. Venetian glass sculpture is extremely popular also and has been for years. Crystal pieces are likewise highly favored by gift shoppers despite their high cost.

- *Pewter and Brassware* pieces are always sought by buyers. Urns, bud vases, decorative mugs, and others are year-in, year-out best sellers.

- *Wall decor* covers an enormous family of products: Mirrors, prints, macrame hangings, hook rugs, needlepoint scenes, clocks, and more. One party plan business woman specializes in lithographs produced by several artists she has under exclusive contract. These are all signed and numbered, and are of great value to art shoppers who frequent her showings.

- *Woodware* encompasses kitchen accessories such as cooking utensils, salad bowls, and goes to hand-carved statuettes for living room accents. African ebony, Danish teak, Colonial maple and walnut lead in popularity, and always find a strong market.

You have a tremendous market here because people are making purchases for their own use and for giving to others on special occasions.

The array of merchandise in gifts and home decor is so large and diverse, you must exercise special caution when you do your buying. The basic points to cover are these: What, generally, are the tastes and preferences of your customers? What is the price category where most of their spending is done? Having an exclusive product line is a perfect target to shoot for, but not at the expense of failing to cater to your customer's needs and pocketbooks.

RELIGIOUS ARTICLES HAVE EXPLOSIVE POTENTIAL, BUT DEMAND SPECIAL MERCHANDISING METHODS

Bibles, religious jewelry and amulets, art reproductions and other items oriented to the church do huge volume figures consistently. This group of products can be marketed with equal success through any of the programs covered in this book.

This category does, however, require a delicate touch with respect to the sales tactics you employ. Customers for religious articles and supplies expect a comparatively low key approach in advertising and personal presentation. As often as not, there is more than an average amount of emotion associated with religion, and thus the consumer is extremely sensitive to the things you say and do in the process of marketing your line.

The emotion factor can also work powerfully in your favor; impulse-appeal is at its strongest, and you probably don't need to do much more than make a minimum effort - in good taste - to get business.

One very good way to avoid being accused of "crass commercialism" in selling religious goods is to know your market. If you are not a member of the faith you are attempting to capture as customers, learn as much as you can about their practices and beliefs. You will be respected for your insight and concern, and you'll be able to avoid embarrassing errors.

HOW CRAFTS RAPIDLY BROUGHT EMILY B. A LIFETIME OF FINANCIAL SECURITY

In the city where Emily operates her direct sales business, if you have a hobby, you buy from her. Emily has an inventory of craft kits so extensive that stores in the area have long since been surpassed in selection.

An average day of calls in a typical neighborhood will gross this enterprising woman at least $200, and yield a net of well over $100. She'll sell an assortment of hobby kits ranging from needlepoint patterns to plastic scale model warships. Her least expensive item is a do-it-yourself doll outfit that retails for less than $2. Her most expensive is a stereo receiver kit that runs $249.95.

Emily's selection is so large, she carries only a few samples along on calls. Her entire stock, however, is printed in a six page circular which she had printed and leaves with customers. Many sales are consummated by Emily on her second visit because she insists that people see the products before they actually make the purchase. This works to her advantage since she'll frequently sell two or three kits of a certain type to the same customer. In addition to the one the person is interested in, Emily brings several others.

In addition to acting as a source of supply for crafts, Emily has also evolved into the position of hobby advisor; when assistance is required by a customer to complete a project, Emily gladly provides guidance. This followup not only assures repeat business, it also gives her extra business in paints, thread, yarn, and all the other items needed to finish kits.

Candlemaking, wood carving, and macrame have been exceptionally good sellers for Emily. But there are literally thousands of craft products she can depend on for future growth and prosperity. As leisure time for most people increases, this woman's business will blossom.

THE LITTLE KNOWN WEALTH OPPORTUNITIES IN BOOKS AND MAGAZINES

In an important way, the success of marketing books and magazines is related to the nostalgia craze discussed earlier. A well preserved 1937 issue of Life magazine can bring its owner back to a different era in an instant. The ads, editorials, and current events of that time can be enchanting to a contemporary reader.

Old books, too, can be treasures. Several merchandisers involved in this unusual specialty have found that the popular childhood novels and storybooks of yesterday are extremely appealing to adults who read them during their youth.

One certain way of capitalizing on the sale of old publications is to have issues available that were originally sold on a customer's birthdate. If a person was born on June 24, 1942, he or she would very likely buy a magazine bearing that publication date. There are used-book stores in large cities that carry huge inventories of these old editions, and many home merchandisers take special orders for specific dates from buyers, then easily find magazines with the required dates in these stores.

Old newspaper headline reprints also fit into this fascinating category. Several firms market a packet of full-size front pages that cover major events and span history back to the Civil War. These are popular for reference or even for framing as wall decor.

While this merchandise category definitely makes good money for a number of people operating home businesses, it is more highly specialized than the others we have discussed and is thus somewhat more limited in terms of market size. It is an effective adjunct to the sale of nostalgia items.

HOW BURT T. FOUND INSTANT SUCCESS IN SEASONAL SPECIALTIES

If you plan to build your merchandising operations around seasonal promotions, you will probably depart from the strategy of confining your product line to one or two categories. Rather than specializing, you will attempt to appeal strictly to seasonal favorites without serious regard to overall item mix.

Burt T. spent six months studying consumer buying trends before he embarked on his own business. He knew precisely which items were most in demand during the key selling seasons. So when he was ready to do his initial purchasing, he knew exactly which items would sell fastest at the biggest profits.

This, Burt admits, is much more of a cold, scientific approach to merchandising than is usually the case. There is no emotion, no individual tastes to consider, and certainly very little attention to trends. Buying is handled by Burt exclusively on the basis of *what sold last year . . . and will it be as popular this year?*

From time to time Burt's suppliers will recommend new products that seem to fit the seasonal appeal he demands in his line. He is very cautious about these and actually buys only a few of the most promising new introductions until they are *proven money-makers*. This conservative but solid philosophy just about guarantees Burt of selling out his entire inventory by the end of each season. Leftovers are minimal, and financial loss due to slow turnover is nonexistent.

Here are the ways to instant success in merchandising only during key seasons:

1. Select the seasons you want to concentrate on. If you'll be operating part-time, you may want to engage only in two or three of the peak times such as Christmas, Easter, and Mother's Day. Or, you might decide to go after all seasonal business which would just about make you a full-time merchandiser.

2. After you pinpoint the seasons, do some thorough research and list precisely the products you'll buy to guarantee success. *Don't* take chances, no matter how great the temptation. Go only with established best-sellers!

3. Get started in your merchandising activities well enough in advance to get you in on the heaviest consumer buying. Being a little too early is far better than getting started too late!

A FEW PRODUCT CATEGORIES TO AVOID

The mistakes which have been made by merchandisers in the past can be invaluable to you in terms of things to stay away from. Certain product categories are inherently accompanied by problems, and no matter how good they may seem to be, they are difficult to handle. The following list describes a few of these problem areas:

1. *Foods* are subject to rigid State and Federal regulations which govern the handling and sale of such products. Aside from these tough rules, there is consumer resistance to foods sold by sources other than established markets. As a result of these two factors, almost every attempt in this area by a home merchandiser has failed.

2. *Pets* are also subject to rules which make sales of animals tricky indeed. The facilities required to properly keep a stock of pets would cost a small fortune, and the merchandising methods described in this book would not lend themselves to the sale of animals. Leave this one to the experts in pet stores!

3. *One-product lines* are any items that you must carry to the exclusion of everything else. For example you might

encounter an arrangement whereby a factory wants you to sell one product they manufacture. Part of the deal requires you to devote all your attention to this item and not show anything else at all. This sort of distributorship might be advantageous to you for a time, but you must be wary about what happens when the item is no longer produced. You'd be left with clientele—but no products to offer them. Your best protection is diversity! The cliche "Don't put all your eggs in one basket" is appropriate in this case.

Now that we've covered the best merchandise categories for home merchandising operations, let's go into a few valuable details about the best ways to buy these products.

10

PRODUCT SOURCES THAT CAN QUICKLY PUT YOU IN THE MAJOR LEAGUE OF MERCHANDISING

THE WORKINGS OF THE MERCHANDISE DISTRIBUTION SYSTEM

Figure 14 illustrates a rather typical movement of goods from factory to consumer. A domestic or foreign factory produces an item (Level 1). If the goods are foreign made, an importer handles the shipping and distribution of the product (Level 2). The merchandise is shipped to a jobber (also known as a distributor). The importer may also act in this capacity, thus saving one level of profit (Level 3). The jobber or importer, as the case may be, gets the item into the hands of a direct-to-consumer merchandiser such as you or a retail store (Level 4).

Level 1.

Level 2.

Level 3.

Level 4.

Figure 14

Remember, the people at every level from 1 to 4 must make a profit. Therefore, it is to your obvious advantage to do your buying as "close" to the factory as possible. If you're the second or third level, it's probably safe. But if you're fourth to handle the merchandise, you are probably not getting favorable prices (unless it's a close-out).

LOCATING FACTORIES THAT HAVE DAZZLING CLOSE-OUTS AVAILABLE AT EYE-POPPING PRICES

Sooner or later, virtually every maker of merchandise will overproduce, make an error in estimating an item's sales potential, or both. A factory might also enjoy a long period of success with a product, then one day phase it out in favor of a new version. In each of these cases, the manufacturer will face the necessity of closing out a certain quantity of inventory.

In many instances, the factory with a close-out will be reluctant to offer its regular customers a cut in price. They may feel that the precedent will make it more difficult to hold a firm price line in the future, or they may view a discount as damaging to their image. (Quite often, brand identification is removed from close-out items.) These particular factories are the ones you want to find out about.

Factory close-outs can be dazzling because you're buying at "level 1" (before products are marked up by middlemen). And even these relatively low prices are lower than usual to attract a buyer. Therefore, it's entirely possible for you to purchase close-outs for prices as low as ten cents on the dollar. An item that retails at $24.95—and usually costs a dealer $10—could be bought for $1!

There's only one good way to locate factories that are sitting on spectacular close-outs: footwork. You must contact every manufacturing firm within a comfortable distance (when a deal comes up, you should be able to get there quickly).

Write each firm a brief letter that conveys these points:

1. You're a merchandiser searching for close-outs.
2. You'll look at anything they have to offer with an open mind.
3. You'll pay cash if you decide to make the purchase.

Send these letters out at least every six months. This will establish you as a legitimate buying source and will keep you in contention for exceptional buys.

You may encounter situations where a factory insists on selling a close-out in one, massive transaction. If they happens to have 8,000 fishing reels on hand, they'd much rather unload them to one customer. It simplifies the bookkeeping and handling considerably. So you might find yourself dealing in rather large quantities as a closeout hunter.

And cash on the barrelhead is a must. There are very rarely extended payment terms on close-outs.

HOW IMPORTER'S PROBLEMS
BECAME BYRON S's DOORWAY TO PROSPERITY

Importing is a field that once belonged exclusively to several giant corporations. But as competition among foreign manufacturers increased, those factories became more and more willing to sell smaller quantities. As the quantity requirements came down, prices went up. So today, almost any individual can order merchandise from distant countries.

As it became easier to import, the field rapidly overcrowded. Hopeful but inexperienced business people made foreign purchases through agents and got stuck with all sorts of merchandise priced far too high to successfully market in this country. Byron S. earns over $40,000 a year bailing out these floundering little importers.

Byron got started in his unique business when a man told him about a shipment of plastic dolls he had imported from a factory in the Far East. When the man first placed his order with an agent, the price of each doll was competitive. But he was not told that the shipment would take five months to arrive, and he was not aware of shipping costs, wharfage, and the myriad other expenses involved in bringing the 500 dolls to America.

To make a bad situation worse for the hapless importer, the market in dolls had softened during the five month wait, and there wasn't a chance he could sell them profitably. He simply wanted to recover some of his cash and get out of the importing business as quickly as he could.

Byron offered the man ten cents on the dollar and finally agreed at fifteen cents. He now owned a shipment of items that would sell at close to normal retail prices through direct sales, party plan, or mail order. But Byron's *profit* would be downright incredible. The dolls were sold within 30 days, and it was just the beginning.

Byron now searches for importers wherever they can be found. He uses the classified telephone directory, Chamber of Commerce lists, and classified ads which he watches regularly. He has learned that while many importers are financially healthy, there are always a few people getting into predicaments like the one he had discovered first. Byron visits them with cash in hand and invariably walks away with unbelievable bargains.

WHERE YOU CAN FIND THOUSANDS OF WHOLESALERS DESPERATE TO UNLOAD DESIRABLE ITEMS

Through full page advertisements in various "how to make money" magazines, several large companies promise to set people up as independent merchandise wholesalers. Among other doubtful claims, these firms tell you that any individual can buy domestic and imported goods from them at prices "well below wholesale."

The fact is, such companies are at the two or three level in the merchandise distribution system explained at the beginning of this chapter. True, they do buy in larger volume and at lower prices than you might be able to, but they still must pay for large advertising and overhead expenses which require a hefty profit margin from the would-be wholesaler who subscribes to their services.

So thousands of well intentioned people fall for these flashy ads every year. They are sometimes required to pay a membership fee for the privilege of buying from firms like these! Then they place orders for general merchandise and hope against hope to market it successfully without advice or guidance and at prices well above most competition.

For every person who manages to eke out a living peddling this overpriced merchandise, twenty-five or more end up getting stuck with their initial stock. The company, of course, refuses to accept returns, so the individual is forced to recover at least a portion of the cash outlay by selling to the highest bidder.

The very best place to find thousands of disillusioned "wholesalers" is through the same magazines that hooked them in the first place. A short classified ad under a category like "Merchandise wanted" should get you plenty of response. Your ad could be worded something like this:

> WHOLESALERS . . . I'll pay cash
> for your surplus products!
>
> Call Jim *(your phone number)*

The publications to use are the same ones described in the chapter about recruiting sub-distributors.

You *must know value* to come out ahead in this particular buying strategy! The person you'll be dealing with is assuredly eager to dump goods—but he or she wants the best possible price, too. So start with an offer of five cents on the dollar and try to keep the final price within fifteen cents on the dollar.

Remember, there are thousands of people who are desperate to liquidate products you can use in your merchandising activities. Be patient and find them!

TAKING ADVANTAGE OF DISTRIBUTORS STUCK WITH TONS OF MERCHANDISE THEY DON'T KNOW HOW TO SELL

Ironically, some of the companies mentioned above, who take advantage of inexperienced people looking for a legitimate business opportunity, can be taken advantage of themselves! They buy as many as 3,000 different items in the course of year, and it's inevitable that a few selections will be losers for them - but potential money-makers for you.

Warehouse space is extremely expensive when thousands of square feet are involved, and no firm wants to have slow-moving inventory taking up valuable room on shelves. Therefore, a distributor who is sitting on a poor seller will want to recover some cash from it and clean it out once and for all.

These particular general merchandise distributors can be found in the same how-to-make-money magazines we have discussed several times before. Make a list of them, and send them letters stating your desire to buy up slow sellers.

Important: There is also a possibility that several of these companies will put you directly into contact with some of their "wholesaler" customers who are stuck with merchandise. This, of course, will save you the task of placing classified ads.

HOW MAX M. REGULARLY HITS THE JACKPOT BY CONTACTING FRANTIC RETAIL STORE OWNERS

A dynamic merchandise source that is too frequently overlooked is the retail store. The average retailer considers business good if he or she can finish a year with a three or four percent net profit. It takes only a few substandard sellers to upset that objective.

The typical store operator is closely in touch with the movement of inventory. Turnover is watched with an eagle eye. When retail customers begin to turn away from a certain product or products, the store owner or manager will usually decide to close them out.

In some stores, a special sale will be held for the purpose of turning slow sellers into cash. Or, the item will be used as a loss leader to bring shoppers through the door. But not all merchants are that innovative or imaginative, so they let the items sit in stock accumulating dust and storage costs. Max M. makes a small fortune finding these frightened merchants.

Max personally contacts at least 15 retail stores every working day. He introduces himself as a merchandise liquidator. He explains that he pays cash for items the retailer wants to get rid of. He will never, under any circumstances, pay more than 15 cents on the dollar, no matter how desirable the product happens to be.

Out of the stores he contacts on an average day, at least three are more than willing to offer Max a superb deal on "tired" stock.

Of these, around half are products the liquidator can use for his own direct merchandising business. But even if Max is not offered a buy when he visits, the store keeps his name and number in case such a need does arise in the future, which it often does.

The enterprising buyer has found that there is very little relationship between the reaction of a retail shopper in a store en-

vironment—and one who is making a selection at a home showing
or from a catalog page. In other words, the fact that the item was
not moving well in a store is no reason why it won't sell vigorously
through a direct marketing method.

Max regularly enjoys gross profits approaching 75% thanks
to his buying technique. And he knows that as long as there are
retail stores out there, he'll be able to buy as much as he needs at a
fraction of regular price.

THE PRO'S AND CON'S OF
SHOPPING AT AUCTIONS

Every major city has a highly active group of auctioneers who
spend a good portion of their time liquidating entire retail inventories. Many of these are bankruptcies and related distress situations that demand the sale of every single item on the shelves.

As a group, autioneers are among the most astute merchandisers anywhere. They know value, they know how to sell, they
understand human nature, and they usually won't consumate a
sale unless it brings a fair price. Therefore, it's highly unlikely
that you'll consistently get the upper hand at auctions.

Your best protection, again, is knowing value. If the auctioneer holds up a folding lawn chair that you *know* retails for
$5.95, and he starts the bidding at $2, you must keep your hands in
your pocket! But if the bidding starts at 50 cents—and you can
finally make the buy at 75 cents, you've got a very healthy deal.

One of the time-honored tricks used by auctioneers is to mix
the excellent buys with indifferent ones. They'll let two consecutive items go at very good prices to soften up the bidders. At
this point, the auctioneer has created the illusion that everything
is a steal. Then the third offer is calculated to bring back the profit
sacrificed on the first two. So the answer is to consider each and
every item on its own merits . . . and *never* bid unless you're absolutely sure of your ground.

Many direct merchandisers feel that auctions do not provide
a sufficient quanity of items—or prices favorable enough—to war-
rant serious attention. Others attend at every opportunity, and
claim to get some of their most important purchases at auctions.

With such a mixed response, your best bet is to try several auctions yourself to see what they can do for you. Attend one or two strictly as a spectator. Learn the procedures and tricks *before* you get into the bidding!

HOW FREIGHT SALVAGE FIRMS
CAN YIELD MAJOR PRODUCT DISCOVERIES

Nearly every time delivery of a truck, ship, railroad, or air shipment is refused by the recipient due to apparent damage to outer cartons, the contents are subject to a freight claim. The insurance company pays the claim, and sells the cartons (frequently unopened) to a salvage firm for a small percentage of their declared value.

The salvage firm is not in the retail business, and is therefore not set up to display the products it has acquired. So they want to rapidly turn around and get a cash profit for the shipment without handling or warehousing. Most of the legitimate freight salvagers know exactly whom to contact whenever they come upon certain types of merchandise. One phone call and the sale is made. *And* it's usually sold at a price few merchants would refuse. But there is a good chance for you to get in on the action.

The key, as in dealing with all other good sources, is to let the salvage companies know you exist. Tell them you'll buy small lots that perhaps the larger outlets don't want to bother with. Eventually you'll get a chance to buy a shipment at prices that make the effort well worthwhile. Persistance will pay handsome dividends.

Watch out for companies which represent themselves as freight salvage operators, but are actually in the retail business. They might purchase a few distressed shipments during the course of a year to make it interesting, but their merchandise is predominantly bought through the same sources *you* buy from. Their price structure—and their eagerness to deal with you—will give them away every time.

It's important to remember this when you shop at freight salvage companies: Surface damage to a carton could mean harm has been done to contents, so if you are expected to make a purchase without the opportunity of inspecting the products, be careful! If it's beyond repair, it's no bargain at any price.

HOW DICK K. MAKES BIG EXTRA PROFITS
SHOPPING THE SHOWS

There are hundreds upon hundreds of merchandise shows held every year in cities large and small. Any product category you can think of probably has several shows that deal with that one specialty. Plus, there are many general shows that attempt to encompass dozens, or even scores, of item classifications.

Merchandise shows were conceived to help manufacturers sell their goods. They are held primarily for the benefit of retail store buyers, merchandisers like you, catalog operations, and anybody else with a need to buy. They are generally set up in large areas like exposition centers, but are frequently held in hotels. Exhibitors rent booths where they display their wares, hand out product literature, and answer questions.

Many shows are closed to the general public. You must prove that you are a bona fide buyer before admittance is granted. Exhibitors are interested mainly in quantity transactions, not in selling one or two items at the retail level. As a direct merchandiser, you shouldn't encounter any problems in getting past the front door.

Dick K. has a group of 20 people operating as party plan sub-distributors. He was invited by one of his merchandise sources to attend a jewelry show to preview the manufacturer's new line, and the experience opened up dramatic new horizons for him.

Dick made the rounds of displays and spent a little time talking to each booth representative. During these visits, he encountered four buying opportunities that gave him tremendous advantages in terms of price and convenience. Here's what they were:

1. A watch manufacturer said he would supply Dick with consignment stock. Invoices would not be payable until items were actually sold by his organization.

2. One factory was showing samples of a discontinued jade line in addition to their new introductions. Dick bought 200 pieces at 50% off prices that prevailed only 30 days before.

3. A ring maker was sampling a new cultured pearl line that was quite different from its usual goods. In an effort to gain fast distribution of the rings, the factory was conducting an introductory special of 25% off regular prices, plus would include free plush display boxes for show buyers.

4. Dick found seven pendants made by a foreign factory that would successfully substitute for fast selling models he was buying elsewhere for around 30% more.

All in all, one visit to a show netted Dick K. tremendous benefits. By his conservative reckoning, this kind of shopping can yield him at least $15,000 *more* in net profits during just one business year! Needless to say, Dick will never miss a merchandise show!

11

BUYING, NEGOTIATING, AND PRICING THE WAY TOP PROS DO IT

HOW HARRY C. GETS ROCK-BOTTOM PRICES BY ALERTLY PLAYING THE OLD RIVALRY GAME

Harry C. is an experienced, hard-bitten buyer for a large general merchandise distributorship. Although you may never have occasion to place orders of the size he does, his methods could nevertheless save you significant money even in smaller scale shopping.

The discovery Harry made that changed his basic buying philosophy was that *there is no such thing as a firm price.* Regardless of how adamant a vendor seems to be, there is *always* a point at which the price will come down. There are undoubtedly

176

buyers who would strenuously disagree, but Harry believes it is true.

In his early buying days, Harry tried everything to get that extra bit of discount. He used intimidation, softsoap, hard luck stories, and others. But the only one that consistently got him better prices was *the rivalry game.*

Harry learned to ruthlessly pit one supplier against another. He would actually create three and four-way auctions that would result in factories bidding against each other to get his business. While this game of Harry's exasperated his sources, it did succeed in getting him what he wanted, lower prices.

When the first price on an anticipated purchase is obtained, Harry immediately calls several other competitive suppliers and states the quantity of merchandise desired, and other specifications. As soon as all price quotations are on his desk, Harry begins to play one source against the other.

If there are four factories in the running, Harry eliminates the highest bidder. Then he calls the third highest and tells the representative that he would consider giving them the business if they would drop the price. When asked how much of a drop would be required to get Harry's order, he tells them he'll call back with an exact figure.

Next, he phones the second highest and tells the representative his quote is outrageously high. At least half the time, the revised price he gets as a result of this call is better than the figure submitted by the initial lowest bidder!

Now Harry contacts the supplier who was originally lowest, and informs the company that they've been beaten, and unless they come through with a much better price, they will lose the order. This is sure to get a price better, or at least equal to, the best quote so far.

The third highest, who was waiting for Harry's call, now has a chance to beat the first two, which in fact often happens. This sometimes triggers a new round of price manipulating . . . all to Harry's advantage. In some cases, the amounts involved seem small, but in the course of one year, they add up to a small fortune.

You can apply this effective technique in smaller scale purchasing activities. No supplier wants to lose an order no matter how small it is. Plus, they realize that in the future your business will be much larger, and the orders you submit will grow proportionately.

THE "IF-AT" STRATEGY RARELY FAILS TO PRODUCE BARGAINS

Much of the effectiveness of Harry's rivalry game is due to the fact that competitors have a built-in aversion to seeing business go to a business rival. But sometimes you may find yourself dealing with sources who have no apparent rivals. In such instances, the If-At system works best.

The If-At strategy is essentially an offer to buy, from you to a supplier. You write a letter that says basically the following:

> If we were to place an order for 288 Toaster Ovens, would you
> be agreeable to sell them at $5.50 each?

The letter itself could be worded any number of ways, but the key points are always there: *IF* we buy (a certain item in a specified quantity), would you sell it *AT* (a specific price you feel is advantageous).

Of course you always want to offer a price that is at least extremely competitive, if not absolutely fantastic. The worse that can happen is the supplier will refuse, or come back with a counter offer. And you can accept it, or attempt to barter a little more.

If-At buying is most effectively done by letter. Personal or telephone contact almost always opens the door for selling and the use of mitigating circumstances which the supplier can use to help justify an upward adjustment of your original offer. You want to keep it simple, and you want to give the source a day or so to think about your offer. The longer he thinks, the more difficult it becomes to turn down business.

One additional wrinkle that a few merchandisers use to enhance the If-At offer is this powerful tactic: You can send a bank draft or check for payment in full along with your letter. That way, the supplier must both refuse your offer *and* return your draft! As you can imagine, one of the toughest things to do is return money to the sender!

TIMING CAN MAKE THE DIFFERENCE BETWEEN BOOM OR BUST

A matter of a few weeks can sometimes make the difference between a fabulous purchase and a very ordinary one.

A supplier's cash flow problems can, in the wink of an eye, turn his entire line into a veritable paradise of bargains. If you keep your ears open, sometimes you can get wind of developing crises in the industry and make the most of them.

Off seasons can also create temporary hardships for factories. First of all, you must find out exactly when various manufacturers are past their peak production months (for the Christmas season, a factory may very well be busiest as early as the preceding February! In November, when the products are being sold to consumers, the plant might be as quiet as a graveyard).

So if a firm has unsold stock after a busy period, your timing would be ideal by approaching them at that time, *not* during the peak season.

These are only two examples of a practically infinite number of possibilities. The most alert merchandisers simply will not make a purchase unless the timing is favorable for buying . . . or unfavorable for selling. These tactics can easily bring you doubled profits.

GETTING THE TERMS YOU WANT

Just because a supplier makes a strong issue of a particular set of terms (say cash on delivery), is no reason why you can't ask for and get 2%, 10 days, net 30 (that means 2% discount from the invoice amount if you pay within 10 days, and the full invoice amount if up to 30 days is taken for payment).

Bargaining for terms that are favorable to *you* is every bit as important as getting the best possible merchandise prices. Good payment terms can give you improved cash flow and thus a generally stronger financial position. Better cash flow gives you the opportunity to buy more advantageously, and it usually clears the way for prompt payment of bills because you have more cash on hand.

Many merchandisers find that their suppliers insist on C.O.D. (cash on delivery) in the beginning of a business relationship. They comply with this requirement (as they usually must do), but never make an effort to get better terms after a solid business association develops. Thus they never make their money work for them as efficiently as it could.

Remember, if you have 10 days or two weeks to pay, you can utilize your cash on hand to the fullest extent before the bill becomes due. You can make other purchases during that period, which you wouldn't be able to do if you had to pay everything on a C.O.D. basis.

One more very good reason for requesting better terms is so you can establish a strong credit rating for your business. If you always pay cash when orders are delivered to you, it will be impossible to establish any kind of payment record that can be checked by vendors in the future.

The best strategy is to conform with the traditional C.O.D. requirement for the first two or three orders you give a supplier. On the next order, try to hold out for extended terms, even if you are granted only 10 days. It's a start.

If you encounter resistance, *push* for better terms. Should the supplier insist on cash, you might go as far as explaining that your future relationship depends heavily on whether or not you get extended terms. If necessary, go to the very brink to get your way!

THE SPECIAL CHALLENGE OF DEALING WITH AGENTS

Merchandisers who have occasion to do their own importing will inevitably deal with agents. These are people who act as the bridge between manufacturers and domestic buyers (you).

An agent usually represents a number of foreign factories. He or she is quite often a native of the country in which the sources are located. These people are generally able to communicate adequately in both English and the tongue of the people who produce the items you want to buy.

The agent, as you might imagine, wants the highest prices possible for the factories he or she represents. Therefore, don't take his first price quotation as final. You must negotiate as hard with an agent as you would with any other seller of merchandise.

Here's an important word that could save you problems in your future dealings: Get to know as much as you can about the culture and customs of the countries you'll be dealing with as an occasional importer of goods. You can drive as hard a bargain as you want, but it must be done in a way that will not offend people of other lands. Any library has excellent reference material on these subjects.

THE WAY DAVE P. GOT EXCLUSIVE DISTRIBUTION RIGHTS THAT EARNED HIM FANTASTIC MONEY THROUGH THE "BITTER/BATTER" PRINCIPLE

In looking back at the deal he made with a major catalog merchandising company, Dave P. admits that he took the kind of risk that most people would shy away from.

With the only money he had to his name, $2,250, Dave agreed to buy the surplus of a high volume firm that annually grossed several million dollars. This firm maintains a line of thousands of items. Every month they have a variety of products they want to liquidate quickly, for cash, to a single buyer.

This was the deal: The willing buyer would get the merchandise for ten cents on the dollar, and sometimes less, but would have to accept *everything* in the surplus category, "the bitter with the batter" as Dave described it. And each month, he had to come up with enough cash to pay for the shipment that arrived at the door of his small warehouse.

Dave took a "roll of the dice," agreed to the terms, and within days received the initial load. It *was* the bitter mixed with the batter! Dave owned perfect name-brand small appliances, beautiful jewelry pieces, fine matched luggage sets, and many other desirable and popular products at prices he simply couldn't believe at first. But he also owned mis-matched bathroom rug ensembles, obscure-brand converters for hand calculators, fifty hard cover books on the art of making paper designs, and so forth.

It takes all the ingenuity Dave can muster, but he successfully merchandises *everything* the big catalog operation sends him. Even half of a skindiver's wet suit on one occasion!

If you have the cold nerve to enter the kind of agreement Dave did, you might be able to work out a similar arrangement with a large company. If you do, it could be worth over $45,000 a year in net income as it is for intrepid Dave P.

HOW GIL F. TURNS DUSTY, FORGOTTEN WAREHOUSE STOCK INTO A PERSONAL GOLD MINE

Two years ago, Gil F. was a retail salesman struggling to make $14,000 a year. Today he's past $30,000, and expects that to jump considerably in the next few months. One simple idea made the difference.

One day Gil was helping the store manager take inventory. After awhile, he noticed that here and there on warehouse shelves were boxes that looked as if they hadn't been touched in many months, perhaps even years. The manager didn't seem concerned about them, but Gil resolved to find out what was in the mystery cartons.

To the salesman's utter amazement, nobody could — or wanted to — shed any light on the situation. Not a single person in the store wanted to be bothered. For all practical purposes, the forgotten items were dead stock. Gil concluded that there were thousands of warehouses that held mystery boxes like these. He decided to make a fortune on this phenomenon.

On his next day off, Gil began to contact warehouses, asking if they had old stock for sale. Out of 12 he visited that day, two offered him special buys on cartons that had been sitting around for years. They were small quantities, but a start. One lot was two gross of imitation pewter ashtrays with assorted sports motifs. The other lot was 50 five-piece glass brandy serving sets.

These quantities were insignificant in terms of the normal traffic at these particular warehouses and therefore didn't justify any special effort at disposal. So the boxes sat and sat. Gil's interest sparked the memory of the warehouse managers, and they quickly got appropriate permission to take a few dollars for the dusty old cartons which held seemingly meaningless items.

Both lots were sold by Gil at big profits by the end of the same week. And by this time he had appointments at 10 other warehouses to look at more tired old cartons that held obsolete contents. The new merchandiser intended to offer ridiculously low sums for each lot, and he fully expected to make the deal in every case.

Within six months, the ex-salesman (he resigned immediately after his first success) had a thriving business going. Warehouses in a 12 state area call him when they want cash for cast-offs. Gil has an incredible knack for spotting gold on dusty shelves!

HOW SMART OPERATORS GET LUCRATIVE CONSIGNMENT DEALS. HOW YOU CAN DO IT

A large number of merchandisers come across situations where they agree to sell products for a percentage of the take. They don't have to buy the items from a factory or distributor; they get a commission when they sell the merchandise to consumers.

As was explained earlier in this book, consignment consists of taking goods to display without buying them. You pay the source only for items that are sold. The unsold stock is returned to the owner.

The distinct advantages in doing business on a consignment basis are these:

1. You don't own inventory, and therefore you can't get stuck with slow sellers.
2. Not owning merchandise, you are able to conserve your cash.
3. Since many consignment deals are offered because items are not selling well, you can usually get a better price on the consignment stock (although some sources will try to get a higher price because of the attractiveness of the consignment arrangement).

In a typical consignment deal, the price you will pay is decided at the time you take delivery of the merchandise. So you know how much you'll have to charge in order to come out with a profit. Therefore, *before* you sign the consignment agreement is the only time to negotiate the best price. You *can't* start price discussions *after* you've sold the products and are ready to pay the supplier!

A few of the toughest buyers ask for consignment terms before they buy *anything!* Even if they know good and well that the source doesn't do business that way, they still ask. Of course they're the ones who most frequently get consignment deals.

Generally speaking, a source will be reluctant to give a total stranger a consignment deal (would *you* hand a stranger several hundred dollars worth of possessions on the strength of a promise?). But when you get to know people, you'll be in a much better position to get consignment arrangements.

BEWARE OF OFFERS THAT LOOK TOO GOOD!

Deals on merchandise that defy the laws of probability can be bad in a number of different ways:

1. The merchandise may be stolen.
2. The goods can be defective.
3. It can be different than represented, such as gemstone jewelry said to be authentic, but actually imitation.

The "laws of probability" are not all that complex: As a fairly experienced buyer, you come to realize that every product can be purchased within certain dollar parameters ranging from low bucks to a top limit. If you suddenly come upon a product that is well under the low mark — and there's no apparent reason why that situation exists — proceed carefully!

True, you'll see close-outs and surplus now and then which *should* be priced under the normal low, but even these opportunities should be investigated before you buy . . . especially if the supplier is not familiar to you. In any event, *always* get a bill of sale from the source and keep it in your files for five years just to be sure.

Not long ago, one very large distributor was offered an especially fabulous buy through an agent. 500 electric hot pots were available for a third of their going price. The buyer for this company could think of nothing else but the gigantic margin he would get on the pots, so he hurriedly made a commitment for the entire lot.

The appliances were delivered 60 days later, and one after another melted itself when plugged in for testing. The entire shipment was defective . . . and thus useless. The cash had been paid by the purchasing firm, and there was no practical recourse to the factory. It was a total loss.

Such are the dangers of buying *too* cheap. And the example above also tells something about the dangers of importing!

GETTING THE SERVICE YOU NEED FROM SUPPLIERS

As long as you plan to exact the most favorable prices and payment terms from your suppliers, why not also demand the kind of service that will help make you competitive with major retail outlets?

Service, in fact, can be every bit as important as price in this age of sharp competition. The decisive edge often goes to the dealer who will most solidly stand in back of his or her consumer transactions.

So you must be positive that with every purchase you make, proper assurance is given by the supplier that the products will perform as they should. If the distributor who was stuck with bad hot pots had exacted such assurances from the agent or factory, considerable grief would have been avoided.

When you import, it becomes a problem to watch out for quality, however. And to depend on manufacturers for service that might be necessary is, to say the least, tricky, when you deal with foreign factories. So to avoid problems, you are probably better off buying from somebody who has already *done* the importing. While you'd be paying a little more because of the importer's profit, you will also have clear recourse to that importer in case of defective products.

When you buy from domestic suppliers, simply be sure of these essential points:

1. If an item is mechanical, electrical, or in some other way must perform a certain function, be certain it works the way it was designed to work. You must be comfortable that it does not represent a hazard since you could find yourself liable if anything happens to a customer due to product malfunction.
2. You should have with each item some kind of printed warranty or guarantee. This usually provides a reasonable length of time during which the product is assured to work — or replacement is made by the maker.

3. With any decorative items you buy, the supplier should stand in back of product quality to the extent that finishes will not deteriorate, stones will not pop out of settings, fabric will not shrink or fade, and so forth.

Remember, it's rarely adequate to settle for verbal assurances from your suppliers. Get service commitments in writing!

THE TWO BEST WAYS TO MAKE ABSOLUTELY SURE YOU'RE GETTING THE BEST DEALS

You can easily do two simple things that will virtually guarantee the effectiveness of your buying. They are basic, yet for some unexplained reason frequently ignored by retail merchants and other merchandisers. Doing them can make your success all but certain in the area of buying:

1. *Get Customer Feedback Constantly*
   The consumer is, finally, the ultimate expert when it comes to price. Yet it's astonishing that dealers rarely pay serious attention to what people say.
   A shopper will tell a business proprietor, "I like that salad set, but I've seen it priced $3 lower." The dealer will too often dismiss the comment as an attempt to get a discount. So nothing is done, and customer after customer is lost because of the price and the seller's indifference.
   Now, almost every home merchandiser or retailer is priced abnormally high on a few items at one time or another. That's not the error. The error is in not making the needed adjustments when there is enough evidence to show that adjustments must be made. Insensitivity like this has been fatal to many enterprises.
   At the very first indication of a price problem in your line, you should make it a point to find out as fast as you can if there's any substance to it. Do this by shopping competitors, searching catalog pages and talking to suppliers. If you can verify that you're being undersold by a significant margin, immediately change your retail prices . . . even if it means cutting your profit to a razor's edge.

If you are successful at proving out-of-line retail prices among your products, take your sources to task. If they're guilty of giving other merchandisers preferential prices, you certainly have a legitimate gripe — and strong grounds for better treatment the next time you place an order. In certain cases like this, suppliers have even been known to issue credits for the amount of the adjustment.

However, if you're up against other merchandisers who buy at the same prices you pay, but are willing to take lower profits — or offering items as loss leaders - you have no choices other than competing or ignoring them. The latter solution can be dangerous.

2. *Keep a sharp eye on what the competition is doing*
A few merchandisers don't wait for customer price complaints. Instead, they spend considerable time watching their rivals. These people don't necessarily mark-up their prices based on a formula of percentages; they go more by what's happening around town.

This system is satisfactory if you have the time and patience to make a science of pricing, but most dealers feel it's an overreaction to competition.

A reasonable approach is to always be ultra-responsive to customer price reaction and to watch your competition for pricing trends that could have a bearing on your activities.

Knowing where to buy and understanding how to obtain the best deals once you get there is good business. In fact, sound business practices will clinch the health of your operation. And you don't have to be a systems expert to master the shortcuts that will make your enterprise a smooth-running machine, as you'll discover in the next chapter.

12

VITAL BUSINESS PROCEDURES THAT BUILD YOUR BANK ACCOUNT AND PROTECT YOUR VALUABLE INTERESTS

EFFECTIVE CUSTOMER RELATIONS

In the first part of this book, we discussed how large retailers were losing ground to smaller dealers who give their customers more personal service and attention. This section tells you how to successfully build customer rapport.

1. *"The customer is always right"* is a cliche we've all heard before. To a certain point, it's correct.

You don't have to take unjustified abuse from your clients, but you must always be civil. If a particularly ill-mannered individual is working on you for no good reason, be polite but firm in ending the association. It may be extremely difficult to restrain yourself under these circumstances, but you *must* resist the temptation of retaliating.

2. *Under certain conditions, you should be willing to lose money if the good will of a customer is at stake.*

   Cases will arise where a customer wants to return an item that has been accidentally abused after the purchase was made. Even though you are sure it was delivered in perfect shape, you'd be wise to graciously make the exchange or give a refund.

   Look at it this way: Refunds and exchanges that will not be supported by the supplier (and thus must be absorbed by you) will very likely constitute around four or five percent of your gross dollar volume. It's just another expense which must be borne by any business. So why not smile while you satisfy the customer? The new business referrals you'll get by using this policy will more than pay for its cost.

3. *But don't be a sucker!*

   If you are asked to make an exchange or refund where willful product abuse or mis-use has taken place, and is obvious, you would be correct in politely declining to make an adjustment. You should be willing to take a loss *only if there is reasonable doubt about why a defect occurred.*

More about putting together an equitable guarantee and exchange program later in this chapter.

APPEARANCE AND RESPECT

The image your business eventually takes on will flow, in large part, from the way you look and act while conducting your activities. A business, as such, has no personality of its own. It merely reflects its owner and employees.

You do *not* need a sparkling and outgoing personality in order to make it big in your business. In fact, more than a few of the most successful people in merchandising are extremely shy and quiet. But they do have one thing in common: Sincerity and respect are the keynotes of their relations with consumers.

Sincerity cannot be projected unless you totally believe the things you are saying. Therefore, a policy of truth in your business dealings will *automatically* create sincerity. When you believe in what you are doing, the customer sense it and feels trust and confidence. But the best actor in the world would find it all but impossible to create feelings of sincerity if there is no basis for it.

Respect can be as automatic as sincerity is. If you take a moment to realize that customers are uniquely different from one another, and each one is a deeply feeling human being, you'll deal with people respectfully without making a conscious effort to do so. You're in trouble the moment you fail to see each person as an entity.

Aside from the way you act toward others, your appearance will also be considered as people make judgments about you and your business. We're in an age where rules about dress are virtually meaningless. Yet this does not provide the freedom to let you wear anything you want. As long as you'll be coming into contact with people from all walks of life, you should attempt to conform to at least a reasonable extent.

Dress is especially critical to a direct merchandiser since business is done in the homes of other people. If you wear paint-spattered wash pants, a prospect would be justified in locking the front door in your face. In contrast, under some conditions a suit or dressy outfit might be too intimidating. So try to find the perfect happy medium and be sure your grooming and cleanliness are up to acceptable standards.

PERSONAL ATTENTION: HOW FELIX P. GOT THE EDGE OVER MOST RETAIL STORES

Let's get into a little more detail about personal attention and how one operator makes it work.

First, just how important is personal attention? This statement by Felix will help put its importance in the proper perspective for you: "If a customer is made to feel that you are putting his or her needs before any other factor, that person will immediately become an incredibly loyal patron, and will tell others about you at every opportunity.

"Translated to dollars and cents," adds Felix, "this means your business can skyrocket; every dollar in volume you would do normally should at least double, and possibly even quadruple, because of the favorable word-of-mouth."

Just how does a merchandiser give personal attention? Here are the rules Felix applies in his own successful direct sales business:

1. The customer must be made to feel important. This is the underlying objective of the merchandiser. This means the customer should get the undivided attention of the dealer until all questions are answered, and all problems are solved. This can be difficult when many shoppers are considering purchases at the same time, but a vigorous effort has to be made to accomplish this goal.

2. Before much of *anything* is done to proceed with the sale, the dealer must ask the shopper questions like these which shed light on individual needs:

   a. Is the desired purchase for personal use or a gift?

   b. What colors must the item coordinate with?

   c. Is there a desired price the customer has in mind?

   There are countless other questions you may ask in qualifying and clarifying the customer's desires. Whatever you do, don't "talk at" the shopper! To do so is a flat rejection of the customer's viewpoint.

3. Find out what the customer's name is, and *use* it. The level of formality you establish will dictate whether or not you use first or last names. Also, encourage your clients to call you by name.

4. *Remember* customer names and other details about them. There is no better way to gain the instant and undying respect of the people who buy from you. The greatest compliment one can receive is to be addressed by name weeks or months after the first introduction.

FOLLOWUP IS YOUR RESPONSIBILITY
AS A SUPERVISOR AND BUSINESS OWNER

Effective customer relations must be practiced not only by you, but by your entire organization—at all times. One sub-distributor who fails to observe the basics we have discussed can undo all the effort you and others are making.

The only way to assure yourself that a solid job is being done is to personally check. This task of monitoring is an ongoing job. It should be carried out on a weekly basis. Here's one very good way to accomplish it:

When new orders are turned in to you by your sub-distributors, you have a record of customer names, addresses, and telephone numbers. You should plan to call at least ten percent of these customers to determine if they are completely satisfied with the way they've been handled. Your sub-distributors should know that such calls will be made by you.

The customers should be asked questions along these lines:

1. Were they able to find all the products they were looking for?
2. Were their questions answered thoroughly and to their satisfaction?
3. Was their relationship with the representative satisfactory?

You are almost certain to make surprising discoveries in the course of these followups. You'll be amazed at how little you actually know about what goes on beyond your sight and hearing! You may find out that exaggerations or outright misrepresentations are being made regarding product performance, delivery time, etc. In most cases, this is due to misunderstanding or poor communications between your sub-distributors and customers, not out of any dishonesty in your representatives (although this sort of cheating is not unknown). Whatever the problem, you'll now be in a position to take action through this followup.

The information you receive from customers will provide valuable clues on where training is needed. As soon as you discover a recurring customer relations problem, you should make it a point to discuss it with the sub-distributor who was involved.

In addition to the obvious advantage of giving you a window to the workings of your business, followup also makes a profound impression on the customer. Does a retail store ever call a customer to ask how everything went during shopping? Not a chance!

ESTABLISHING YOUR COMPANY CREDIT IS A BIG STEP TOWARD DYNAMIC GROWTH

Establishing a line of credit with suppliers is as simple as paying them when your bills come due.

You do not have to be involved in million dollar transactions to build a solid reputation for taking care of your obligations. For example, if you do business with a certain manufacturer to the tune of only $200 a month and the invoice is paid promptly month after month, it strongly demonstrates your good ethics. Then, when you apply for a substantial loan for the purpose of expansion, merchandise, or other worthy reason, the lending institution will take your record into account, no matter how modest the amounts may be.

A previous section of this book told about how to get extended payment terms from your sources. That's the first step, and an absolutely necessary one. If you remain on cash terms, you'll never be able to prove that you honor your commitments since you won't *have* any commitments.

When your new suppliers are able to contact your existing suppliers and get references regarding your payment record, it will usually get you a line of credit sufficient for average size purchases (a "line of credit," in this discussion, means up to 30 day terms).

But if you plan to borrow an unusually large sum, the lending institution will probably require you to sign a personal note. In other words, your business will need *your* backing in order to qualify. This is true of large businesses and small ones alike. It is no reflection on your status.

On the other hand, a corporation (as opposed to a sole proprietorship, as you would probably be as a home merchandiser) *can* stand alone in a borrowing situation without guarantees of private individuals. But corporations have certain drawbacks as well as advantages. These will be covered next.

SOLE PROPRIETORSHIP, CORPORATION, OR PARTNERSHIP: WHICH IS BEST FOR YOUR PURPOSES?

You have a choice of these three ways to set up your organization. Most often, a new enterprise falls into the sole proprietorship category; you're an individual doing business without a partner and with little or no supporting staff—at least at first (subdistributors are considered independent contractors, and not employees).

In the comparatively simple individual proprietorship mode, you are required only to obtain a city license (generally around $20). This enables the local government to determine the legality of your operation and its conformity to zoning laws. The other necessary step is the registering of your company name if it's fictitious (for example, Ajax Merchandisers—if your name is actually Robert Jones). This is usually done at the same time you get your city license. The people at city hall will advise you as to the proper procedure.

As a sole proprietorship, you have virtually total freedom of movement. Much more so, in fact, than you would have as a corporation or partnership. And, as mentioned earlier, establishing credit requires that the owner personally sign for business loans. This also means that you are personally responsible for any debts incurred by your business, whether it continues in existence or not.

A corporation is an entity. This means shareholders are in no way responsible for the organization's debts. Shareholders can be your friends, relatives, or anyone else who buys or otherwise holds shares of ownership in your company. Many small corporations are closed—where shares are not offered for sale to outsiders, but are held by family members.

A public corporation, however, offers shares in the business to anybody willing to invest in them. This is a very good way to raise capital for expansion, but the danger is always present that somebody will buy a controlling interest and take over the company. There has been more than one instance where the founder and owner of a firm found himself on the outside looking in! This can't happen in a sole proprietorship.

A corporation can be established by contacting the Secretary of State in your state capitol and requesting the needed forms. It's a complex procedure, and you should have the assistance of legal counsel. Costs can run up to $1,000 or much more, depending on location, complexity and other variable factors. When your enterprise begins to produce huge income, it may be time to convert to corporate structure.

A general partnership is advantageous when two people desire business success, but each individual excels in a different area of the operation. You, for example, may be good at conducting party plan sales, and your associate may be adept at mail order. It sets the stage for a successful partnership.

Or, you may form a partnership with a financial backer; you have the skill, he or she has the money to make it go. This can be a limited partnership in which case the other person does not actively participate in day to day activities, but remains vitally interested in the profit picture.

Articles of Co-Partnership must be drawn up in the process of establishing a partnership. In this agreement, the precise terms of profit division are spelled out, as well as details about how assets would be apportioned between partners should the business be discontinued by them.

Again, a lawyer should be consulted if you plan to set up a partnership. When two people are involved together in an enterprise, the chances of dispute are ever present, and every facet of possible disagreement should be clearly delineated in the Articles of Co-Partnership.

MONEY CONTROL POLICIES THAT HELP YOU AVOID FINANCIAL RISK

Many successful businesses run into disaster because of weak or nonexistent money control policies. At year's end, State and Federal taxes must be paid; accounts payable (money you owe to suppliers) must be known at any time, as must credits due you from suppliers.

If a customer's check is returned to you marked "not sufficient funds," or if a cash remittance is misplaced, you should have the ability to quickly find out where the original sale is and precisely how much money is involved.

A system that will show the general health and overall progress of your business is *essential!* And it is not at all complicated to start and maintain.

Almost any major department store or business supply store sells single-entry bookkeeping systems at very reasonable cost. The instructions enclosed with such a system can be mastered in an hour or two, even if you have absolutely no prior experience in accounting.

Quite a few merchandisers use local business services to handle their money control. A brief visit once every two or three weeks is sufficient for such a service to bring entries up to date. The cost is nominal and well worth it. They take your day to day sales receipts and expenditures and make journal entries which reflect the pulse of your activities. Journals can show payables, receivables, profit & loss, and other valuable financial information. So there are basically three ways you can go:

1. You can obtain a simple, single-entry bookkeeping system and keep both daily records and the journals which will be required when tax time comes.
2. You can keep just the daily records and let a local business service work on the journals.
3. You can let a business service do everything for you.

The Internal Revenue Service will want you, as a business owner, to make quarterly tax payments along with an estimate of your next quarter's earnings. This rule is designed to protect self-employed individuals (who don't have employers making withholding deductions from their salaries). With the quarterly tax payment system, you won't get a huge tax bill at the end of the year.

A visit to any Internal Revenue Service office can rapidly clarify the quarterly payment procedure. They'll give you the required forms, and show you exactly how to complete and submit them. Or, if you decide to use a business service (or a private accountant) to keep your books, they can easily handle this tax work for you.

However you decide to handle the keeping of sales and financial records, you are strongly urged to do it at the very outset of your business activities. This will assure you of having a clear and complete picture of your growth and freedom from worry about the proper handling of tax payments.

HOW HAROLD L. CONTROLS EXPENSES
WHILE IMPROVING OPERATING EFFICIENCY

There are countless temptations to lure a business operator into overspending—secretarial help, office equipment and elaborate printed materials are just a few. As soon as a cash surplus shows on the books, many operators succumb to the lure and immediately spend it.

Even the thriftiest merchandisers should work with self-imposed restraints on spending. You and your accountant (or business service) should arrive at budgets for every aspect of your business. You would be wise to instruct the person doing your books to establish *extremely tight budget limits*.

In almost every instance, a tight budget will teach you to get much more efficiency out of every profit dollar. You'll learn to squeeze every last drop out of your allowed expenses. This kind of thinking will, in time, become habit. Then, when you begin to prosper, economy will be second nature to you.

Early in the life of his business, Harold L. found it necessary to resort to stringent money conservation policies. He started on a shoestring and feels that his ultimate success was due to the saving habits he developed in those first lean months. Here are a few of the measures he took to stretch precious cash:

1. Harold arranged his sales visits, and also his calls to suppliers, by geographical location. He always planned to spend a given day in one locale, getting as much accomplished in this area as he could. This provided tremendous savings in automobile expenses and his personal time. Harold estimates a monthly saving of at least $45.
2. Harold never discarded the packing materials sent by his suppliers with incoming merchandise. It was carefully

stored until Harold needed it for his deliveries to customers. Thus, he rarely needed cartons, insulating materials or paper. Estimated saving each month, $15.

3. When this starting merchandiser received business correspondence, he saved paper clips, unused envelopes, manila folders and other supplies of that sort. The result was a dramatic reduction of his need to purchase these items. Estimated monthly saving, $10.

4. Each time Harold had to get printing done, he'd spend an extra few minutes getting competitive bids. He would also look at such things as alternative paper sources and other cost cutting methods. The low bidder was invariably 10% to 20% lower than the highest price. Approximate monthly saving was $15.

5. One small investment Harold did make was $10 for a used but accurate postage scale. It saved him, on a daily basis, the errors that usually accompany guessing about the weight of letters and packages he sent out. Therefore, he never overpaid on postage. Estimated monthly saving, $4.

These measures alone saved the new businessman a neat $89 per month. There were other economies that sent the figure up over $100. To a beginning enterprise, indeed a significant monthly sum.

But more importantly, the habits Harold established have carried through to this day. His business is thriving and is more complex than it was in those days, and the savings now come to over $500 a month!

SETTING UP A GUARANTEE AND EXCHANGE PROGRAM THAT KEEPS CUSTOMER LOYALTY AND BUILDS YOUR VOLUME

We've already discussed the importance of giving customers assurance that you stand solidly in back of your products. Now we'll go into a few specifics of how to build a program that's both fair to you and equitable to your customers.

1. *EXCHANGES*

    If you decide to allow customers to exchange one item for another, you must explain your policy regarding these points:

    a. The length of time they have in which to make such an exchange (usually measured from the date of delivery).

b. Requirements as to the condition of the item the customer wishes to exchange.

2. *RETURNS*

There are many legitimate reasons why a buyer might wish to return a recent purchase to you. The person may develop "buyer's remorse" which is simply a change of mind some time after delivery is accepted. Or a husband or wife might disagree with the selection. At any rate, you should be prepared to deal with returns based on these guidelines:

a. Again, a time limit should be set.

b. Condition of the item to be returned must be taken into consideration.

c. You must determine whether you'll give the customer a credit toward a future purchase or a full refund for the product.

3. *CANCELLATIONS*

Your state undoubtedly has "cooling off" regulations under which a customer may cancel an order. These rules apply to all direct sales operations, and thus can affect your policies. So the first step is to find out from the State Attorney General exactly what the rules are.

A cancellation occurs when an item has been ordered by a customer, but was not yet delivered for one reason or another when a change of mind occured. When delivery *has* been made at the time of purchase and the buyer later wishes to cancel, the transaction is properly classified as a return.

In the former event, a deposit has probably been submitted to you. The disposition of that deposit has to be resolved by you; will you refund it to the cancelling customer, or agree to apply it toward a future purchase? The answer depends on your final policy and on what you find out about the state laws governing direct sales.

4. *GUARANTEE POLICY*

Almost everything you sell should be accompanied by a statement describing to the customer the guarantee policy which applies to that particular product. A 19¢ keychain obviously would not be subject to a guarantee, but any costly item should be.

For example if a watch is sold, the buyer would get tremendous comfort knowing that if it failed within 30 days, it would be replaced. If it developed a problem beyond 30 days, but within 90 days, a $5 charge would cover any necessary repairs. These figures are used only for illustration, but are rather typical.

The specific guarantee terms you offer would stem from the arrangements you agree upon with your various sources of supply.

A SURE WAY OF MAKING BUSINESS DOWNTURNS PRODUCE INCREASED VOLUME FOR YOU

Most business operators live in mortal fear of slumps. The average operation simply doesn't possess a cash reserve large enough to carry it through a spell of reduced sales and profits. So when inevitable downturns come, thousands of these firms are forced to permanently cease operations. In direct-to-consumer merchandising, however, you have built in protection against this eventuality.

First of all, when business activity dips, sub-distributors become especially plentiful. The employment market slows considerably and more qualified people are job hunting. Thus you should have a field day selecting representatives.

Ironically, slowdowns don't seem to have much of an effect on sales of low-priced merchandise to consumers. Perhaps they maintain their buying in order to keep their spirits up. When financially pinched, people stop purchasing automobiles, major appliances, and other large scale products. So for home merchandisers, it's business as usual during recessions.

The combination of sub-distributor availability and strong sales during downturns gives you an ideal climate for making record money. As soon as a slump hits, go all-out in hiring representatives!

TAKE BIG TAX BREAKS AS A BUSINESS OWNER

Tax laws strongly favor people in business for themselves. Part of your residence can be used for your work and can be deducted. A portion of your telephone bill—that part chargeable to customer contact—can be deducted. There are many, many, other ways to save important tax dollars in addition to these.

The key to taking advantage of all legitimate deductions is to keep daily records. A simple booklet, available from most stationery supply stores, provides space for entering these continuing expenditures.

Consultation with your local Internal Revenue Service office can be enormously helpful in getting advice about which figures to be concerned about. A private tax service can supply the same information. This input can make your planning more effective, and can save you significant money at year's end.

WHAT TO DO WHEN YOUR BUSINESS OUTGROWS YOUR HOME

If you follow the steps in this book, you will certainly come to the point where your home becomes hopelessly inadequate as a base for merchandising operations.

You may find that telephone traffic justifies a second phone. Or mail volume may come to surpass the ability of the Postal Service to deliver it conveniently. But the biggest problem, warehouse space, could easily become the main hurdle to continued home operations.

When you arrive at this delightful juncture, by all means resist the temptation to rent plush offices and huge warehouse facilities! A company which requires frequent visits by customers and suppliers can justify large expenditures for fancy offices, but *you* need *working, functional* space, and it can be modest and nominally priced.

Another point to remember is this: *Avoid* signing long-term leases! Numerous offices are available on a month-to-month basis. You never know when you'll be ready to expand again, and you don't want to be tied down by an obligation to occupy certain quarters for a year or two.

Quite a few merchandisers in the midst of strong growth find that a desk, telephone, and file cabinet in a one-room office serve the immediate purpose. An answering service can be obtained at low cost. They'll take all calls during business hours while you are out where the money is.

The acquisition of warehouse or storage space should also be approached conservatively. Rent only the amount of space you actually foresee needing in the *immediate future*. Don't try to peer too far into the future. Since space of this sort is generally easy to locate and obtain, it's almost always available on very short notice.

By now you might be deeply involved in the first stages of your home merchandising career. You have more than enough knowledge, more than enough assurance that you can easily handle it, and plenty of facts about where to obtain goods. It's only fitting that at this point we discuss how far and how fast you can go.

13

HERE'S JUST HOW RICH YOU CAN GET

BOB K. TELLS ABOUT HIS THRIVING NEW ENTERPRISE

"I've worked for maybe a dozen different companies in my life. With every employer, I gave everything I had to give. There wasn't one job where I didn't make lots of money for my boss. One day I just got tired of beating my brains out for everyone else. I finally had the confidence to do it for myself. In eight months I had more money in the bank than I ever had before in my life. I'll never work for anyone else as long as I live!"

This man's statement is typical of what most people would say who have ventured into their own home merchandising businesses. *Individuals who start and prosper in their own enterprises are NOT better, smarter or luckier than you!* They simply come to the point where they take the step and DO it!

This new merchandiser *immediately* began to enjoy the same success he had experienced during the years of working for companies. Bob's initial move was to get people to do the work for him; after all, if *he* eagerly toiled for others in the past, why wouldn't people be willing to work for him now that *he* was a boss? In a matter of weeks, six new representatives were working for Bob's young business.

In the first year Bob made a personal income of just over $43,000. But the most exciting thing were the doors which suddenly opened up for him as a prospering business owner. He now sees a side of life he had no idea existed earlier in his career. The concluding pages of this book describe a few of the opportunities that came along for several prospering merchandisers.

HOW ERWIN B. GETS THE UPPER HAND
EVERY TIME HE MAKES A BUSINESS DEAL

Erwin freely admits he doesn't care much for the day to day running of a business. Besides, he has found a way to make at least $75,000 a year without even worrying about the details of daily operations!

As often happens when people are in business for themselves, Erwin unexpectedly came across the formula that would provide him substantial income. Here's how it happened:

Erwin started a home merchandising business just as anybody else would do. He combined direct sales with mobile showroom merchandising and got off to a quick start. In three months, the new dealer's earnings were at $1,950 net per month and surging upward. At this point, Erwin received a proposition that changed his business career.

During a sales call one day, the woman Erwin was visiting asked him what was entailed in starting a merchandising operation like his. He briefly explained a few details, then the lady asked if her husband could call him later that evening for more information.

That afternoon, Erwin gave some thought to what a business like his was worth: If he could expect to draw a net income of around $25,000 the first year, then a total price of about $30,000

would be a bargain to a buyer. That would be just a little over one
year's income to the new owners.

The woman's husband called Erwin that evening. It turned
out that he was an accountant and, as Erwin expected, itching to
make a career change. He had been fruitlessly looking for a small
business that he could buy for a total of no more than $35,000,
with an $8,000 down payment, the balance to be paid from profits
over a period of time. He was immediately interested in Erwin's
company, so a meeting was arranged.

The deal was signed, sealed, and delivered at their third
meeting. The attorneys for both sides were present, and the
accountant handed Erwin a check for $8,000. It was the largest
sum he had ever possessed at one time, and he felt like a millionaire.

Erwin agreed to provide 30 days of training, plus another 30
days of consulting services. After the intensive training period,
Erwin set about starting another home merchandising business in
a town far enough away to avoid any conflict with the one he had
just sold. Within four months, he found a buyer who agreed to
purchase the new operation for $25,000!

Today, Erwin starts and immediately sells party plan, mail
order, mobile showroom merchandising, and direct sales businesses. He finds that people are in the market for *going* concerns
where income is coming in, a certain amount of customer good will
has been established, and inventory is on-hand. He knows that as
soon as he produces his books for inspection by a prospective
buyer, the deal is as good as made because of the immediate
profits he gets when he starts the business.

Erwin easily starts and sells three businesses a year. And that
nets him an easy $60,000, plus the income he makes during the
start-up cycles!

HOW TO SELL YOUR THRIVING ENTERPRISE
AND KEEP ALL THE ACES IN YOUR HAND

Some people who start and sell home merchandising businesses prefer to completely break away from the enterprise once
the dotted line is signed. But a few remain involved and add even
more to their mushrooming income.

There are a number of interesting arrangements you can make with a new buyer that will provide continuing profits for you. Here are the most typical ones:

1. *Consulting*

   Many new business buyers want ongoing advice until they are on their feet in terms of running the operation by themselves. Since you've been through all phases of the enterprise, there is nobody more qualified than you to fill that role.

   Such a clause in the sale of your business to another might call for two, six, or eight months of contact with the new owner. The amount of time spent each week is specified in the agreement, as is the total length of time you will make yourself available for guidance.

   Your fee for supplying experience and expertise should be in a range that will not place unreasonable financial burden on the business. Yet you must realize that the time you spend will not be productive in the development of new businesses. Consulting fees can range from a low of around $15 an hour and go as high as $70 an hour or more.

2. *Merchandise Brokering*

   A few merchandisers have worked out plans whereby the purchaser of the business continues to buy products from the former owner. This opens the door to several intriguing possibilities, and some that are not so advantageous.

   On the positive side, the new owner is free to devote time almost exclusively to developing new business. There is no concern over locating sources and negotiating with them; it's all taken care of by the former owner, who takes a fair profit for the effort of acting as supplier.

   The negative aspect of this is that the business is acquiring goods at a somewhat higher price than would normally be the case. And he or she is also insulated from the buying function which could hamper growth in the future. But this arrangement, too, could be for a limited time. At the end of, say, a one year period, the buyer could be introduced to all sources and be "set free."

   Brokering can create a fabulous wealth opportunity for you. If you have started and sold several home merchandising businesses, you can rather easily set yourself up as a buying cooperative; in other words, you become the central purchasing authority for a number of independent businesses. This can give both you and your clients enormous volume purchasing power. Co-operatives really can offer the small business person some of the benefits enjoyed by giant firms.

A cooperative service of this nature would be a permanent enterprise that would require your continued participation.

3. *Being Careful About Contract Restrictions Can Make Big Extra Money For You*

Each time you sell a business you have started, the buyer will undoubtedly want some assurances that you will not go into competition with him as soon as the ink on the bill of sale is dry.

When a prospect wisely does insist on a clause limiting your future merchandising activities, you can benefit significantly by being firm with regard to what you agree to. The main thing is, don't paint yourself into a corner by agreeing to refrain from direct sales if the only business you started and sold was mobile showroom. And think carefully before you consent to not operating within a 500 mile radius if your town is only four miles from border to border.

Only the business you sold should be subject to any kind of restriction. And the area you agree to stay away from should be reasonable, and in fair relationship to the size of the city in question; if your effective marketing area covers 50 miles, *don't* agree to refrain from doing business within a 100 mile radius. Finally, the time limit on the restriction should also be reasonable. Five years is certainly excessive, but one year seems good for all concerned.

JETHRO M. TELLS HOW THIS MERCHANDISING KNOWLEDGE EARNS HIM $75 AN HOUR . . . WHEN HE FEELS LIKE WORKING

There are other ways that people turn their home merchandising expertise into big money. And as soon as you have gained a little experience, you can do the same things.

Jethro M. started a direct sales operation at age 55 — after an illness forced him to leave his job as an assembly line foreman. He worked at building a following for three years, then decided to sell his business and retire. After only one year of leisure, Jethro was ready for more action.

The retiree considered starting another direct-to-consumer business, but decided it would be too much of a personal commitment at his age. Instead, he felt that his experience and record of success could provide good money in consulting. And he would work only when he felt like working.

The first step was to gather a list of every home merchandiser he could find out about. Jethro's former suppliers were extremely cooperative in providing the names and telephone numbers of people who bought from them; the vendors understood that if Jethro's consulting services could increase the business of their customers, purchases would grow larger.

Having collected the names of 32 merchandisers in a four state area, Jethro began calling them. He introduced himself, described his experience and success, then offered a consulting package deal that was extremely appealing; he would work with the business owner four hours a week for a period of four weeks. His flat fee for this time was (and still is) $1,295.

His price works out to $75 per hour, plus $95 for travel time and incidental expenses. Jethro tells his prospective customers that if, within the first two hours, they do not see the enormous benefits in this guidance, there is no obligation to complete the deal, and the time spent so far is not charged.

After two years of consulting, Jethro M. has succeeded in bringing substantial increases to the businesses of his customers. He is now traveling the entire western U.S.A. serving over 30 clients. He earns $36,000 a year easily, and takes it slow.

WHAT TO DO WHEN YOUR WORDS AND IDEAS ARE WORTH A MINT: THE STORY OF CHARLEY G.

Jethro M. discovered that his background was worth hard cash through consulting newer merchandisers. He "sold what was in his head", so to speak, rather than buying and selling merchandise. Charley G. also utilized his extensive knowledge of direct-to-consumer sales, but in a slightly different way.

After six years of conducting a successful party plan and mail order business, Charley found himself prospering, but with very little to do. Almost every function of his operation was being ably handled by employees — except making the deposits which Charley especially enjoyed doing himself. He hungered for new activity — and found it. He was amazed at the additional income it brought him.

It started when Charley was invited by one of his daughter's teachers to speak to a group of high school seniors about his business activities. He prepared an outline, practiced speaking in front of a mirror, and was soon ready. His talk, originally scheduled to run 30 minutes, turned into 90 minutes. Charley's address was so informative and well-delivered, the group wouldn't let him leave the stage!

Charley had actually astonished himself by the depth and breadth of his grasp on the subject of merchandising. He now had total confidence that he could teach other adults the tricks and secrets of making big money in businesses of their own.

The first step was to plan a one-day seminar at a local hotel. Charley rented a banquet room and proceeded to advertise for attendees. The day would cost $20 per guest, and he planned to limit attendance to 30 people. Eighteen guests enrolled, and the day was successful far beyond his expectations. The gross take was $360. Charley cleared $283 that day!

It gained size and momentum like an avalanche: ads ran three time a week; attendance grew to 40 each session, and the fee went up to $50 per guest. Charley's average gross was a whopping $1,600!

In addition to his seminars, Charley found himself in tremendous demand as a guest speaker. His fee for a dinner talk of one hour was $250! His total income, including the continued profits of his still growing home merchandising business, is now just over $85,000 a year!

WHAT YOU NEED FOR HUGE EARNINGS

There isn't a single case history related in this book that couldn't describe *you*. There isn't an income quoted that couldn't be *yours* a year from now, or even sooner. There isn't one strategy that you can't make happen tomorrow if you really want it to.

You now have every bit of knowledge you need to propel yourself to huge earnings. You have every tool, every resource at your disposal. And you have a huge, affluent market surrounding you, ready and willing to buy and keep buying.

The seeds of accomplishment and wealth are in *every human being on earth.* The ones who make it are the ones who believe in themselves, who give themselves the chance. They refuse to listen to the millions of losers who say "it can't be done" to everybody who will listen to such discouragement. Instead, they follow the winners. Then they discover that the rich are no better, no smarter, and not a bit luckier than anyone else.

These new winners also learn, sometimes to their utter amazement, that *life gives them exactly what they ask for.* So they put an absolute stop to the business of thinking about why they *shouldn't* have this or that . . . why they don't *deserve* the finer things . . . or why it's noble to deprive themselves of everything they dream of possessing. They begin to *expect* good things, and good things do begin to happen!

This is much more than "having a positive attitude." It's a real down-deep conviction that you *are* better, smarter and more deserving of absolute success than you have ever believed before. This belief in yourself is inside of you right now, and you must let it come to the surface without delay.

When you experience the unbelievable thrill of completing a day in your own home merchandising business with $200 cash in your pocket, you'll truly understand the kind of self esteem and pride described above. And from that first, small step, there won't be any stopping you until you reach the heights you want for yourself, that you so richly deserve!

Index